Schmidt's Anatomy of a Successful Dental Practice

Schmidt's Anatomy of a Successful Dental Practice

by Duane Arthur Schmidt, D.D.S.

DENTAL ECONOMICS

PennWell Publishing Company
Tulsa, Oklahoma

DISCLAIMER

Neither the author, nor PennWell Publishing Company,
stipulates that any legality mentioned in this text can be applied to any other state,
or to any other dental practice. Please consult with your attorney,
accountant, insurance agent, or management advisor before applying any
concept or document discussed in this book.
The ideas contained herein are conceptual only,
and under no circumstance can be construed to be legal advice.

© Copyright 1996 by
PennWell Publishing Company
1421 South Sheridan/P.O. Box 1260
Tulsa, Oklahoma 74101

Schmidt, Duane A.
    Schmidt's anatomy of a successful dental practice/by Duane Arthur Schmidt.
        p.   cm.
    Includes index.
    ISBN 0-87814-585-0
        1. Dentistry—Practice. 2. Dentistry—Practice—Anecdotes
    I. Title.
        [DNLM: 1. Practice Management, Dental. WU 77 S349s 1996]
    RK58.S374   1996
    617.6'0068—dc20
    DNLM/DLC
    for Library of Congress   96-33681
                                                                                CIP

Printed in the United States of America by PennWell Books

1 2 3 4 5 00 99 98 97 96

OTHER BOOKS
BY THE AUTHOR:

The Late J.C.

3 Steps to the Million Dollar Practice*

Earn More/Work Less*

Hands On: Dental Computers Made Easy

Iowa Pride

Published by PennWell Books

DEDICATIONS

To the memory of my colleagues:
Alton K. Fischer, Don Griffith, Bill Goodale, Bill Mellerup,
Frank Molsberry, Herbie Hoover, Bob Hufford, Leroy Larsen,
Doug Nelson, Arne Oosterhuis, Jerry Schekel, Jim Trask, Bill Simon,
Ken Wessels, and brother Bob Williams.

To my associates:
Jim Knight, Masih Safabahksh, and Jeff Akey,
and the incredible staff at Gentle Dental.

To friends who have enriched my life:
Charles Blair, Christine Dahl, Terry Goodman,
Arlen Lackey, Bob Margeas, Linda Miles,
Omer Reed, and John Wilde.

Dedicated, as always,
to Dianne, Cyd, Catherine, and Brigitte.

ACKNOWLEDGMENTS

Many thanks to PennWell Books editor Kirk Bjornsgaard
for coaxing this book from me, encouraging and prodding me to be my
best me. Thanks, too, to *Dental Economics* publisher and editor Dick
Hale for being my great friend, coach, inspiration and associate.
Third-book thanks, once again, to my friend and editor Laura Browne
who, as my Great Barrier Reef, protects me from sharks and shoals,
and most of all, from myself.

All names used in this document are fictitious.
The events, however, are all real.

CONTENTS

PREFACE

"Duane, there's a guy in my office who claims you roughed up his little girl this morning."

I sucked in my breath and collapsed into a chair.

"Oh, my God!" was all I could gasp into the receiver.

Bill Sanders, Wilber County attorney and parent of two patients in my new pediatric dental practice, was a friend. Friendship, however, can't save a man from drowning in a current this treacherous. My mind froze on the vision of the *St. Albans Chronicle* front-page headline-to-be. Surely it would scream, "Dentist Accused of Battering Three-Year-Old!"

In my mind's eye, I saw my new practice shatter, and bankruptcy, shame, and ignominy trash my fresh professional career. In an instant, I saw my dreams dive out the window and splatter on the concrete, five floors below my Carver Building office in St. Albans.

"Who, Bill?" I finally managed to ask. Six months earlier, I had opened a dental practice in this northwest Iowa town of 30,000. The area had never experienced the services of my pediatric dental specialty. My office was roughly 350 square feet in size and contained one dental chair,

four reception-room chairs, a couple of magazines, and one employee—
me. Within a few months, the practice expanded to two chairs and I hired
Kay, who was to become my trusted receptionist for all 14 years of this
practice.

After four days of waiting for my first patient, the phone finally rang
and slowly my practice inched alive. Word-of-mouth, from professionals
like Bill, spread through the right circles of town, soon bearing fruit. In
those days, the Iowa Dental Health Plan operated all over the state, and
school nurses, delighted to have a pedodontist in town, became fine
referral resources.

Around town, and in adjoining counties, a large population of
nearly-retired dentists eagerly purged their practices of child patients.
My practice presence was a godsend to those senior dentists.
Capitalizing on this truth, early every Wednesday morning I drove off
in a different direction from St. Albans to make friends with my
colleagues and hope for referrals. In whistle-stops like Manson,
Humboldt, Pocahontas, and others, I opened lines of communication
with scores of senior dentists.

As specialists are inclined to do—for obvious referral reasons—I
jumped at the offer to preside over our local dental society. There, I
worked hard to gain friendships and colleague acceptance. Early fears
and doubts about the wisdom of choosing a town as small as St. Albans
in which to practice my specialty began to abate. I had a young family,
huge debt, jumbo dreams, immense determination, and, at the moment,
a mouth full of cotton.

"Who is she, Bill?"

"Jennifer Rice. Her father's got blood in his eye and wants a pound
of flesh, Duane."

The squalling little face came back to me and I recalled the trial her
appointment had been. She had bawled from the reception room to the
operatory and back again. She left the office a sobbing, tear-stained,
protesting possessor of a new restoration.

"Yeah, we saw her all right. Cried like sixty. You know how small
my office is, Bill. Her dad heard every tear. Heck, lots of kids cry in a
dental office. Everybody knows that," I rambled, trying to make sense of
this senseless accusation.

"Duane, I know that, but he's got some damning evidence."

"What evidence?" I was quite sure that my heart stopped beating.

"She's covered with bruises. Got 'em all over her arms." A desperate situation spiraled downward into a black hole.

I was stunned, too numb to think. I simply sat and stared. Time ticked on and Bill listened to the silence. Suddenly, my adrenaline kicked in, my mind began to function. There had been something unusual about Jennifer's appointment. What was it?

"Wait a minute, Bill," I said. Dropping the telephone receiver on my desk, I ran to my files and dug for a certain chart. There, I retrieved a prize and held it up.

"Yes!" I yelled into the phone. "Bill, I have proof I didn't harm her."

"What kind of proof?"

"You know those new Land cameras, the ones that develop a picture on the spot? Don't they call them Polaroids?"

"Yeah. That's right."

"I got one for graduation. Over the weekend I came up with my big idea. If I offered to take their picture, maybe crying kids would stop and smile. Then I could win them over."

"And?"

"Don't you get it, Bill? Jennifer is the first patient I tried it on, but my plan fell flat. I kept her snapshot, though. Didn't want to give her a picture of her crying," I said. "Do you know what, Bill? Those bruises show plain as day. She's sure been beat up, but it happened before she ever got in my office. Ask her father about that!"

"Get me that picture right away, Duane."

"You bet!"

Kay sped from the office and I listened to my heart throb like Longfellow's, "muffled drums . . . beating funeral marches to (my) grave." In a few minutes, the phone broke in. I scooped the receiver to my ear.

"Duane, Bill. You should'a seen his face when I showed him the picture. I told him I was considering filing child abuse charges against him. The creep got his butt outta here plenty fast!"

"Thanks, Bill." I was too weak to say more. The phone tumbled into its cradle.

Fast-forward forty years.

Lucille seemed normal enough, but her hands were quietly shredding a rather nice lace hanky. Earlier, my chairside assistant had warned me about this distraught patient.

"We've got a lady with a serious problem in chair three, Dr. Schmidt," my assistant said.

"Really? How so?"

"She says her last dentist planted a radio in her tooth. Now he's listening to all her thoughts!" She let the impact of her words sink in, then continued. "Her last dentist did a root canal filling on number eight. The 'radio' is supposedly hidden in the lingual composite." The assistant shook her head in disbelief.

I thought I had encountered every possible circumstance in dentistry, until now. We went to the chair.

"Lucille, this is Dr. Schmidt. He's going to . . . uh, help you with . . . er, with your problem." My patient looked up with pleading eyes. She started to speak, but I held a finger to my lips.

"Hello, Lucille. Yes, yes, I know," I said, nodding knowingly.

We gave her a large mirror, which she positioned just inches from her nose. She then watched us quickly pulverize the filling in the lifeless tooth. The intrusive radio perhaps was destroyed in the process, but it was difficult to tell for sure. Lucille closely inspected the scoured cavity and seemed satisfied.

"It's gone," I softly reassured her. "Your thoughts are safe. No one can ever listen to your mind again." Her shoulders lowered by inches.

By now, the composite was mixed. I held the material between my fingers, so the operatory light shone through it.

"See? Pure plastic. No radio." She nodded and, defying technique, I quickly pushed the composite into the cavity, with my gloved hand. When the restoration had set and was polished, Lucille hugged my arm, thanking me profusely for her mental salvation.

From the chilling crisis with Jennifer to the tragicomic episode with Lucille, my 46-year dental career has been a graying process— accumulating gray hairs and exercising gray matter, simply to survive. We're going to talk about that.

It All Began When . . .

I began my stand-up dental journey as a belt-and-pulley, mortar-and-pestle kind of dentist. There were no chairside assistants. We plied our practices in a solo, lonely profession, at ungainly chairs, bending our spines and psyches out of shape. When things got too tough, we simply lit up and blew smoke rings.

We knew that dentists earned more than their share of hemorrhoids and varicose veins. Who cared? Everyone knew that dentists led the professions in alcoholism, divorce, and suicide. So what? We wouldn't have traded places with President "Ike" Eisenhower.

There was no vacuum suction at the chair. Instead, swirling water softly swished bacterial contaminants around the rim of a chairside spittoon. Our numbed patients drooled strings of saliva into what we fondly referred to as our "gahboon." We resharpened and reused anesthetic needles. We washed our patient bibs. There were no disposables.

The highest handpiece speed barely reached a few thousand revolutions. Cheap steel burs dulled quickly and were sent off to be resharpened. Enamel removal was such a chore we chose gold inlays over full crowns. Patients self-administered nitrous oxide until they passed out and dropped the mask. During lunch, the odor of blood from morning surgeries lingered on our fingers, scenting our sandwiches.

There were no dental advertisements, no practice management experts, almost no management books, and little animosity within the dental community. Lawyers were our friends and golf partners, not our adversaries. Then, dentists fought side by side, entrenched to eradicate the world's most prevalent disease.

No third-party carriers ruled our roosts. The government ignored us. We all belonged to the ADA. Boards of dental examiners were composed of colleagues, compassionately caring for the public trust, not the "good old boys" they were later vilified to be.

Times were certainly different.

Then one day, the profession awoke to find our patients horizontal. Fellow Iowan John Naughton, with prodding dentists Barney Morgan and Meigs Jones at his elbow, devised a new age of lie-down dentistry. Den-Tal-Ez salesmen taught the ins and outs of multi-hand, vacuum-fueled, turbine-driven dentistry.

Then one day, "nine old men" of the judiciary intervened, in *Bates vs. Arizona*. Uncle Sam's all-knowing minions declared the nation to be dentally bankrupt, and dental colleges geared up for grants and grads. Eagle-eyed actuaries espied profits, and insurance companies jumped into our newly-acquired cash registers. OSHA flexed bureaucratic muscles, becoming lawmakers by fiat.

Seemingly overnight, dentistry became a business, relevant and retail. Internal and external marketing experts sprang out of the woodwork to teach dentists how to mastermind their checkbooks. Dentists stole patients, bad-mouthed each other, and the profession struggled to maintain balance, a sense of direction, and a nobility of purpose. Honor and ethics somehow were steamed away like viruses in the autoclave of commerce.

Through it all, while marveling at the privilege of watching the panorama, I made one more discovery: My trusty mission statement was woefully deficient.

I had believed in, and operated under, one of Benjamin Franklin's knowing maxims. After all, hadn't so many of his other aphorisms been true? "God helps them that help themselves." "Time is money." "A penny saved is a penny earned."

Ben's adage that did me in was woven into the wool of the Midwestern work ethic, which was my first carpet. It went, "Early to bed, early to rise, makes a man (before gender parity) healthy, wealthy, and wise." Eureka! It worked!

I went to bed early; rose with the chickens; ate, drank, and exercised judiciously; and did indeed become wealthy and wise. However, the wisdom I learned was not quite what Benjamin Franklin had in mind. I learned that James Thurber said it better, when he paraphrased, "Early to rise and early to bed makes a male healthy and wealthy and dead."

Thurber was far more prescient than Franklin. For, though I acquired much of the wealth that Ben Franklin spent a lifetime kiting and courting, I also became worn out, tired out, and burned out. So, I sold out and got out—a dental dropout. I was finished in dentistry, washed up at 40 years of age. A statistical burnout, I was trashed by the profession I loved.

Between my terror with Jennifer and the tragicomic episode with Lucille, a great deal of saliva has flowed under the rubber dam. I've banged pretty hard into both walls, going down the dental hallway of life.

Wherever most dentists have practiced, I've been there. Those stops included graduate school, a teaching assistantship, military service, and practice as a dentist associate, solo specialist, solo generalist, and multi-doctor practitioner.

Whatever size most dentists have known, I've been there, too. Those sizes ranged from my first cubbyhole, solo private practice, to my current 8,000-square-foot, 23-chair, 36-member, electronic dental office. I guess you could say that I've been around the block and stopped at all the corners.

To escape the caper with Jennifer, all I had to be was supremely lucky. Imagine taking only one picture of a patient in 46 years of dentistry, and that picture turning out to be the one that saved me from professional disaster. To deal with Lucille only took compassion.

Between those two events, I've gathered some hefty scars. Sexual harassment charges? Been there. License suspension? Done that. Office drug thefts? Oh, yeah. Fines from the U.S. Department of Commerce? To be sure. Six-digit losses in outside investments (all were sure things, to be sure!)? I plead guilty. IRS audits? Yes. IRS line audits? Yes, indeed. IRS criminal audits? Yes, of course. OSHA inquisitions? You betcha. Peer review? Yep. Associate lawsuits? Why not? Small claims court? Sure. Jury trial for malpractice? Yes, to this and all the above. As columnist Dave Barry says, "I'm not making this up."

To survive—yes, even prosper—through this mishmash has taken some gray hair and some gray matter. Colorists claim that there are 29,000 shades of gray. *Schmidt's Anatomy* is all about some of those grays.

The stories are not all pretty; certainly they are not self- serving, but they are brutally honest. Honesty is always its own reward. Consider the dairy farmer and the baker.

A farmer sold one-pound tubs of butter to a baker. After a time, the baker suspected the tubs did not always weigh a full pound. When he weighed them, he confirmed his suspicions. He found they often weighed several ounces under a pound. When he reported his findings to the police, the farmer was hauled before a magistrate to answer the charges.

"What do you have to say for yourself?" the judge asked.

The farmer looked at the baker, swallowed hard, shook his head, then answered, "Your honor, I am a poor man, trying to do an honest job and make a living for my family. Because I have little money, I do not own a scale to weigh my butter."

The baker looked to the judge and smiled a smug "See-I-told-you-so!" smile, then settled back to await what he perceived to be the farmer's confession.

The farmer continued, "However, I do have a balance beam, your honor. Every morning I buy what the baker labels a one-pound loaf of bread. Then I weigh out enough butter to match its weight, before my family eats the bread."

The stories you are about to read are honest. They contain a full pound, measured on scales, not a balance beam.

Two decades ago, and several years after my dental flameout, I returned to dentistry, fired with a new mission statement . . . one that works. I'll tell you how we dealt with those crazy circumstances, how we escaped serious injury in the process, and how we have taken steps to prevent a recurrence. For me, once was enough. For you, once is too much.

Let's start with a mission statement that works.

CHAPTER ONE

EMBRYOLOGY

"There are two things to aim at in life;
first, to get what you want; and, after that, to enjoy it.
Only the wisest of mankind achieves the second."
—LOGAN PEARSALL SMITH
AFTERTHOUGHTS, 1931

When dental students labor over Anatomy 101, they sweat through the classic medical text, *Gray's Anatomy.* I don't presume to trade on its prestige or detract from its awesome content. However, the pattern of that anatomical concept offers a nice metaphor on which to base this *Schmidt's Anatomy.*

Assembling a successful dental practice closely resembles the manner in which a human body is put together. The parts must all be there, whole, sound, and functional. A missing part portends a problem, just as in a dental practice. For example, when the staff does not obtain timely informed consents, those missing parts—like absent ears or eyes— mean possible problems.

The analogy, however, from the real *Gray's* to this *Grays* can be carried too far. We who wrote, edited, and input these pages won't let that gratuitous event happen. There's another reason. While the anatomy of a dental practice is important, the function (physiology) and the malfunction (pathology) of parts is no less important.

THE EMERGENCY NIGHTMARE

Take the example of a dentist who runs a well-constructed and successful dental office. One day he returns to the office after hours to serve a patient. The next day the dentist's world caves in, for he is charged with sexually violating that patient. That happened to a dentist friend of mine. An incredible career crashed on one bad judgment.

This scenario represents a breakdown in the *function* of an office which, in this instance, has nothing to do with this office's organizational anatomy. Prudent dentists *never* return to the office alone. A dentist who risks returning to the office alone demonstrates functional office illiteracy.

Why? Because a population of druggies, psychopaths, and bad people is intent on plunging into a dentist's pocket. Emergency philanthropy, in today's new world, makes no sense. This does not mean we abandon our patients. We probably serve them better with a 24-hour answering service, referral to a 24-hour emergency medical facility, and by employing 24-hour prescription drug facilities.

The last after-hours emergency I attended happened one cold fall night, five years ago. I was reluctant to go, but the caller implored me in a voice so honest, so convincing, so trustworthy, I could not deny him. Against my better judgment, I yielded. Fortunately, I first called the police, told them the circumstance and asked them to meet me at my office. They promised to send a squad car at once.

My first look at my patient, sauntering in the shadows near my office door, confirmed to me that I had made a bad judgment call. However, at that moment, going along with his request seemed the better option. I unlocked the door, and, as we entered the office, I asked him what his problem was. He carefully spelled out his demand.

"Doc, I need a prescription for 36 Tylenol 3's right now. Just do that and there'll be no trouble."

The word "trouble" carried all the signals I needed to tell me that this was not a normal office call. As steadily as I could—not knowing for sure what he held in the hand jammed into his jacket pocket—I answered, "I'll write your prescription, pal, but let me tell you what's going to be waiting for you outside that door. I always call the police when I come down to the office at night, and at this moment a squad car is driving into that driveway behind you."

All I saw, in the next instant, was his backside making fast tracks out of my office, racing away into the blackness. The police car was where I thought it would be. The officers understood, chuckled (this was *not* funny!), congratulated me for calling them, and made out a report. I went home knowing the final piece of wisdom I needed to handle my patients' future emergency dental needs: Be a telephone dentist after hours.

HIDDEN EXPOSURE

Here's another example: A dentist, working in an anatomically fine office, opens the mail one day to learn that he or she is charged with sexually harassing an employee. We can so easily be blindsided by people and events we never suspect.

Fifteen years ago, the letter that then upended my world read, "Dr. Schmidt, unless you promptly remit $15,000, we will file charges against you for sexually harassing your former employee, Ms. Twyla Bendell. Ms. Bendell reports that you told her that unless she had sex with you she would be fired. Further, we will file charges of sexual harassment on the job with the Iowa Civil Rights Commission." I understood every syllable of what seemed to be a coercive letter.

Twyla's attorney threatened to file a lawsuit and civil rights charges unless I forked over the dough. His premise was simple. Unless I paid up, he would publicly humiliate me. A lawsuit is a public document, and cannot be hidden. Some governmental bodies pursue charges such as this, because of what they deem to be their deterrent value. They rarely seem to suspect that some bad people simply do evil things, like lying.

Newspapers, under the principle of freedom of the press, print unproven lawsuits or charges, pontificating that the public good is served by letting people in on charges (Fig.1–1). This attitude ignores the reality that the person charged is permanently damaged the minute the unproven charge is printed.

I fail to understand how the public good is well-served by printing charges that have not cleared the court system. Who dreamed up a "freedom of the press" that means one person can harm another human being with an unproven charge?

Is it important to warn of peril, when the peril is unproven? The publication of unproven stories convicts the subject by implication. You will believe that statement when you are the subject. Public humiliation was employed in puritanical days to whip sense into people. Only the naive believe those archaic stocks have been left in our past.

If you think for a moment that this cannot happen to you, I invite you to realize that letters like I received will be opened by a significant number of dentists this year. What's a significant number? One, if it's you. Can't happen to a female dentist? Please rethink that outmoded belief.

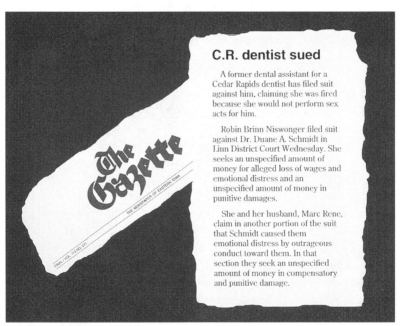

C.R. dentist sued

A former dental assistant for a Cedar Rapids dentist has filed suit against him, claiming she was fired because she would not perform sex acts for him.

Robin Brinn Niswonger filed suit against Dr. Duane A. Schmidt in Linn District Court Wednesday. She seeks an unspecified amount of money for alleged loss of wages and emotional distress and an unspecified amount of money in punitive damages.

She and her husband, Marc Rene, claim in another portion of the suit that Schmidt caused them emotional distress by outrageous conduct toward them. In that section they seek an unspecified amount of money in compensatory and punitive damage.

Fig. 1–1 News clipping of sexual harassment charges made against Duane A. Schmidt, D.D.S.

Before we return to the mission statement, let's wrap this sexual harassment episode. I promised at the outset I would be honest with you. It opens a bit of a wound to discuss this—particularly in a public document—but the facts have all been printed in the newspaper and are in court documents, so hiding them helps no one.

Here are the facts and what I did. You tell me what I should have done. We were in the middle of a busy Friday morning at the office, when a long-term staff member came to my private office and asked to speak to me. I asked Geraldine to come into my office and close the door.

"Doctor, we are having a problem with Twyla."

"How so?"

"She is always late, in the morning and at lunch, and she never stays to close up at night."

"Why haven't I been told before?" I knew the answer. The staff, as a good team will do, had covered for Twyla, hoping to get her to change her ways. I did not fault them for trying to salvage one of their own, so I thanked Geraldine for her honesty. "Let me check her time cards, and I'll let you know what I'm going to do."

An hour later, I learned that Twyla had been late 93 times since she began her employment, about six months before. I called her into my office, closed the door, and asked her to produce her key, gather her belongings, and punch out. I told her she had some good qualities that I would stress if anyone called me about her employment with us and thanked her for her past work.

A few days later, we received a notice that she had applied for unemployment compensation payments. At the hearing, I showed the examiner her time cards. She failed to show for the hearing and was denied all benefits.

Within a week, her attorney's letter arrived demanding reparations for her imagined sexual harassment wrongs. At the time, we employed three doctors, three hygienists, two dozen staff members, and were growing nicely, heading toward $1.5 million in production. Fifteen thousand dollars would not have broken the bank.

What would you do—buckle to the coercion or fight the case? It was not an easy call. I'm a hard-headed German. I fought. Within days, the obligatory news release announced the filing of the lawsuit. The publicity was, as expected, humiliating.

Be aware that professional liability insurance does not protect or defend against sexual harassment charges. The cost of this defense came out of my pocket. My attorney filed interrogatories of questions we wanted answers to. Since we had committed to fight the charge, we were fully prepared to take the case to trial. The interrogatories went unanswered and we never heard another word from Twyla or her attorney. Her attorney never filed charges with the Iowa Civil Rights Commission.

We received a judgment that never was reported in the newspaper. Twyla left the state and was never heard from again. In the pathological real world, should this happen to you (God forbid!), your local newspaper will report, "Assistant Alleges Local Dentist Demands Sex For Employment." This is a trial and conviction in the press, without benefit of giving your side to it.

The American Dental Association should place top priority on lobbying efforts to change the law so only people who are convicted of crimes are reported in the press. Newspapers and attorneys will fight that concept tooth and nail, for a variety of reasons.

Once a suit is announced, guilt or innocence has nothing to do with anything. Irreparable damage is done. The charge becomes both sentence and conviction. No amount of public relations, retractions, withdrawals, denials, or even winning the suit will assuage the connotation of guilt that hangs forever over that dentist's head. This instance represents office pathology at its worst.

Listen up. I'm telling you the truth. No gender is immune. No dentist is safe. Each of us practices pathological peril. Just as any of us, for whatever reason, can contract a cancer, so dental office pathology happens. There are ways to create barriers, lessen the risk, and prolong a happy professional life. They are worth knowing.

Rule Number One: Never (ever, ever) visit with an employee without another employee present.

"But," you protest, "that is a totally impractical rule for my office." You continue, "Our staff has worked together for years and we are like family. My staff would be insulted, if I didn't have private talks with them. Blah, blah, blah."

Sorry, I can't hear your protest, for our office employs almost three dozen women, many of whom have been with us from 10 to 15 years.

We have taken trips to Hawaii, have cruised together in the Carribean, gone to Cancun together (Fig. 2–6), attended office parties together, and still . . . I am not so slow as to believe that a problem cannot occur. I refuse to talk with any staffer without another person present. Period. You should, too.

Would you like me to describe what a nice young lady Twyla was, how sweet, how gentle, how childlike, how vindictive, how much knowing her cost me in psychological stress, actual practice loss, and dollars to my attorney? You don't want to know those things, but, believe me, they are part of the equation.

How do my staff and I talk when the situation absolutely demands privacy? It's really quite simple. We merely turn on the tape recorder and I talk into it, in front of the staffer, stating the date, the time, and that I am taping it with the employee's knowledge and consent. The team member then speaks an agreement, after which we tape our conversation. That's a very simple precaution

Rule Number Two: Every three months all staff members are required to sign a document stating they have not seen sexual harassment of any sort nor have they been sexually harassed during the past three months. There were a few other statements we'll talk about later, as those topics arise (see Fig.1–2).

Rule Number Three: Expect the unexpected. That means take nothing for granted. Whatever I've told you here has not been enough. I wish I knew it all.

A PROPER MISSION STATEMENT

For now, I'd like you to start reviewing the embryology of dental practice by writing down exactly what you want from dentistry. Take a piece of paper and write down your goal. If the paper is larger than an appointment card, your goal isn't well defined.

Mission statements that trail on for paragraphs or pages, are useful as tools of the process rather than the product. For example, a staff/team may get together to define the office goal in precise words. This exercise can be either highly useful or futile.

Team Member's Statement Of Knowledge

OSHA

I have been instructed in OSHA policies, rules, regulations and practices by being personally taught by the office Exposure Control Manager, who is a trained staff member, by reading required and appropriate materials, and by observing the American Dental Association OSHA video. I understand these materials and state that I know of no violation of OSHA rules, currently or in the past year, at Gentle Dental.

Financial

I know of no instance where any doctor or employee at Gentle Dental has charted any circumstance that did not occur exactly as charted. I know of no fraudulent billing of a patient, an insurer or Title XIX. I know of no funds received in this office that have not been reported for tax purposes.

Prescription Drugs

I know of no instance where drugs have been prescribed for nondental needs either for patients or for staff members at Gentle Dental. I know of no instance of drug abuse either by staff members or doctors at Gentle Dental.

Dental Assistant Duties

I am trained in the duties that are allowed to be legally performed by a dental assistant (or by a dental hygienist, if appropriate) and state that I have not performed any illegal duties. I have not been asked to perform illegal duties and I have seen neither other dental assistants nor hygienists perform duties that are not allowed under the license laws of Iowa. I have not known of anyone at Gentle Dental asking an assistant or hygienist to perform an illegal duty.

Sexual Harassment

I understand the Gentle Dental office policy forbidding sexual harassment in the workplace and state that I have never seen, heard or known of a single instance of sexual harassment occurring at Gentle Dental either by staff or by doctors.

Fig. 1–2 Release statement signed by all staff members.

On one hand, the staff is inspired to think, interact, and define the vision. The problem is, staff vision may be so lofty that it has little meaning. A goal of "staying on time" doesn't mean a whole lot. Subconsciously, this goal may alter awareness, and possibly result in some behavioral change, but it's doubtful.

On the other hand, a useful goal might state "we will bring every patient to the chair within 10 minutes of entry into the reception room." This goal, followed by specific ways to get the job done, just might work.

My Statement of Free Will

While I have been asked to make this statement by the staff of Gentle Dental, I state that I make these statements of my own free will. I have not been coerced or forced to make them under the threat of losing my job or reducing my salary or hours.

I further understand that I have been informed that I may report future violations of any of the above circumstances to various state and local agencies.

I further agree that if any dispute about the terms of my employment, my performance on the job, any claim of harassment, discrimination, or any other claim whatsoever shall arise, during or following my employment, it shall be submitted to arbitration under Chapter 679A of the Code of Iowa (1993). It is understood by both myself and Gentle Dental that by agreeing to submit all claims or assertions that either Gentle Dental or I may have against the other, arising out of this agreement, Gentle Dental and I have given up our right to a jury or a court trial.

Signed _____ Dated _____

Witnessed _____ Dated _____

Subscribed and sworn to me this _____ Day of _____, 1995.

_____

Jean M. Corey, Notary Public

© 1995, Success Press

Fig. 1–2 *(Continued)*

To reach this level of insightful result, someone must virtually guide the process as it develops. That's a heady task most people would avoid. It's tough enough to reach our own conclusions, to say nothing of helping others reach their answers. The problem is, the end result may indicate more of what the doctor wants than what the staff feels possible.

Staff goals will usually express altruism at its finest. That's okay, I suppose, but altruism in the dental office—at least, in the few offices I've seen it at work—becomes things like morning prayer meetings and group-bonding rites.

Those procedures can have value in some offices. A fine management group in Ohio and Indiana inspires its clientele to sensibly use motivational morning meetings for the team that seem to make sense.

The normal office simply tries to stay afloat, which is an admirable pursuit. Most offices haven't gone to the woods to make a staff mission statement. Few offices have morning charge-up sessions. The majority of offices, in my experience, simply take the doctor at his or her word and go for it.

That makes the doctor's mission statement even more important. I've already told how a mission statement of merely making money was inadequate. It is still as worthless now as it was then. One of the main reasons that going for the gold doesn't work—besides its own vacuousness—is that it deals the staff out.

The doctor who fails to include staff in goal-setting has some serious beginning work to do. Go back to *3 Steps to the Million Dollar Practice* (PennWell Books) for starters. If a doctor is to achieve what he or she wants, the doctor must learn that the most important member of the team is the assistant.

Then what mission statement brought me back into dentistry? The answer is fun to tell you about. It's fun because the answer is just that—fun. At the outset of my new practice, two decades ago, coming back into dentistry off a really bad flameout, I decided that I would do two things:

1. Never have a bad day, as long as I lived and

2. Have fun every day of my practice.

The program works!

HAVE A SOOPER DAY!

In the late 1970s, I heard of this new-fangled contraption called a computer. In Iowa, we had seen stories in the *Des Moines Register* about how Iowans John V. Atanasoff and Clifford Berry had invented the digital computer. Not many people, me included, realized the portent of this invention.

Iowa State University failed to file for a patent. Imagine that loss, if you can. Atanasoff created this monster just before World War II began. After the war—as a witness for large companies—he was involved in a $7 million legal battle with a fellow (Mauchly) who tried to steal his glory. Atanasoff was declared the inventor. We, who read about it at the time, vaguely knew the computer could do things that humans did, only faster and easier, and that it never asked for a sick day.

Then, a hard drive cost well into six digits, meaning few people had one. Maybe there was one in Iowa, maybe not. I heard there was one in Minnesota, though, and when I learned that a fellow by the name of Jim Trask resold time to dentists, I called and we signed on.

He called his business a service bureau. Following every dental procedure we performed in the office, we wrote what was called a super bill, containing the patient's name, account number, and procedure code. At the end of the day these were batched and sent to Minneapolis for processing.

There, keypunch operators input the data to the patient's financial ledger. At the end of the month, statements went to our patients and a continuous form of our ledger accounts was sent to our office. When patients called about their accounts during the month, the business receptionist could quickly look up the account and give correct information. We thought the system was about as nifty as sliced bread.

It was at this time that I picked up on the idea that the computer was like a brain, and the brain was like a computer. Both accepted input, the computer from a keyboard and the brain from our senses. Both processed the information according to programs. The computer utilized software programs that instructed the central processing unit (c.p.u.) how to process the data—add it, subtract it, correlate it.

The brain processed data much the same way, according to programs. Where the computer received its programs from instructions someone had thought out and placed on a disc, the brain received its programs from its genetic markers, cultural influences, schooling, and sensory input. This knowledge led to the point that if the brain was like a computer, able to react to data input on the basis of its programs, why not change the programs so the brain would always conclude that a positive day—call it sooper, as I did—was to be had for the asking. Made sense to me.

Not only did this simple reprogramming effort make sense, it worked! The minute I installed this program, I failed to have any more bad days. I knew what those days amounted to, had experienced too many of them, enough so I knew I wanted no more.

How does the program work? First, there are a million programs in the world that want to reprogram mine. Mine won't allow anyone but me to reprogram it. Outside sources are continually trying to enter my program and reprogram me. Who? You know who they are—zealots, tinpots, cranks, angry people, demagogues, politicians. The question is better asked, who is *not* trying to reprogram me to suit their ends?

Patients are among the worst offenders, constantly trying to reprogram us to their wishes. Our office policies are set in stone. They are fair, and we do not intend changing them for anyone. When a patient says, "Your assistant told me . . . ," and I know it was not what she would say, I always *support* the team member. New patients are a dime a dozen. Good staff is tough to find.

Several years ago a patient began swearing in the chair. His disruptive and obnoxious behavior annoyed everyone within earshot. Another doctor in the office was in the process of treating him, but that doctor was in his private office. I walked over to the foulmouthed patient and asked, "What's the problem, buddy?"

He erupted into a stream of profanity, whereupon I reached down, lifted the arm of the chair, grabbed his arm in a vice tight enough to blanch fingers, and said, "Come with me."

As it became apparent that we were headed out of the office, his profanity increased in volume and intensity. Walking by the front desk, I asked my receptionist to call the police. At that, he broke away from my grip and raised his hands above his head, preparing to crash them down on my head.

That movement is not a smart move against a person who owns a black belt in Tae-Kwon-Do karate. He picked himself up off the grass outside and we never heard again from our foul visitor.

It is okay, all right, perfectly fine to fire a patient.

Another patient bit into my finger as I opened his mouth to examine his old dentures. I pulled off my glove and realized he had broken the skin. I was outraged.

"What was that for?" I asked.

"Oh, I was just having a little fun," he declared.

I lifted the arm rest, grabbed his arm, and walked him to a side door. "Have your fun somewhere else, pal. The human bite is the most dangerous of all, and we just don't think your humor is funny at all." I shoved him out the door and we went on with life, happy that we did not have to deal with patients who refused to deal on our terms.

Life is not long enough to endure recalcitrant patients.

The first few years of my pedodontic practice taught me another important lesson in that regard. In those early 1960s, the door to my reception room held a sign that declared, "Cowboys and cowgirls, check your guns and parents at the door." Most people accepted the message and obeyed it, but one day I received an intercom message, "Doctor, would you step out here for a minute, please?"

The message came through loud and clear. There was either a parent who wouldn't stay in the reception room, or a child who couldn't leave it. The problem was rarely anything else.

"Dr. Schmidt, this is Mrs. Wickham and her daughter Guenevere." I spoke to both and shook hands with Guenevere, who had tightly wrapped herself against her mother's leg, hand, and arm. The situation was obvious. Kay filled me in that Guenevere was a new patient, and her mother did not believe in my policy of no parents in the operatory.

Neither person knew the story of the time when I allowed a parent to watch a procedure, back in that first cubbyhole office. A few minutes after the mother came into the operatory, I heard a clunk, and looked down to see the mother lying on the floor. The child immediately began to cry, and I was faced with the dilemma of trying to revive mother *and* calm her child. Never again.

Dentistry has never been a spectator sport and those who allow operatory visitors take on more liability than I ever want to see.

"No, Mrs. Wickham, we do not allow parents in the operatory. You see, I am working with sharp instruments and a sudden movement—if a child suddenly would try to relate to a parent—could be dangerous. I just won't take that chance."

She grabbed her poor child's arm and nearly jerked it from its socket. "Dr. Schmidt," she leaned into my face, "I'm going to ruin you." Nice, friendly lady. I looked at Kay, as Mrs. Wickham dragged her hapless child from our office, and suggested that she start looking to find us both new jobs.

We thought no more of the incident until a few weeks later, when my receptionist told me, "Doctor, the phone is ringing off the hook with new patients."

"Where did we go wrong, Kay?" I asked in jest.

"Do you remember Guenevere?" she asked. I remembered. Ruin is not a word one forgets. "Well, her mother is honest. She is telling all over town how we won't allow parents in the operatory and people are calling and saying, 'Is this where parents can't go back to the chair?' When I say 'yes,' they make an appointment and say, 'Finally there's a dentist who doesn't need me!'"

There are other ways that people try to reprogram us. Our supplier may back-order something I think should be in stock. Our laboratory may miss a seat date. My staff may forget to schedule an important event for me and fail to mark time off. Patients constantly want to reprogram our office policies, my staff, and me. To all the above we simply say, "No thanks," and go about having sooper days.

Here are some real-life reprograms and how we deal with them. My receptionist announces a call on line four. "G'd Moanin', Doc-tor Schmee-idt. How're yew to-day?" For some reason these pitchmen all seem to sound like English is their second language, if that. When people call so solicitously concerned about your welfare, can't you spot a sales pitch, usually for a donation, a mile away?

"What do you want, friend?" I ask. He sputters, says he doesn't want anything, then proceeds to tell me what he wants. Often his spiel goes something like this: The local Ragpickers Society is having a charity Country and Western show at the coliseum and, knowing how much I care about small children (I could be a pedophile, for all he knows), he wonders how many tickets he can put me down for "so the po' liddle, unnerprivileged chil-dren will git ta see this wunnerful show."

The thought always occurs to me that the little children may end up being even more underprivileged for having seen his show, but I resist the temptation to say so.

My stock answer goes like this. "Tell you what, my friend. I've got some charities of my own, so here's my offer. You write a check to me for $100, which I guarantee will go 100 percent to underprivileged children with uncared-for dental needs, and then I'll match it with a check to you for the same amount. Deal?"

Sputter, sputter. "We-ll, now, Doc-tor Schmee-idt. That there's a right gen'rous offah 'n I'll tek it up with mah frens heer and we'll git back to yew." Not likely, friend, but he's programmed out of my life, and it was sort of fun doing it.

Another. "Dr. Schmidt, I got this fantastic new job selling advertising on golf scorecards!" I know what's coming next, but I own the reprogramming program, so I lead him into it.

"Gee! That's great, Bill. With your skills, you should make it really work out well."

"Do you think so? Well, how much can I put you down for, Doctor? Boy, there's thousands of people who are gonna see these scorecards every year. You ought to get a whole lot of new patients from advertising on them."

I know full well I could put my office name on every tee, give out free golf balls, and surround the course with billboards and not get a single patient from them. Instead I answer, "Oh, gee, Bill, you just missed it." I give him my best crestfallen look.

"Missed what?" He stares at me wide-eyed.

"The committee meeting. They meet every year, my lawyer, my accountant, and my office administrator, and they go over all advertising proposals and set the budget for the year. But don't feel bad. Just give our office administrator your material, and she'll see that it gets thrown in the hopper for next year."

Gently let down, he nods agreement, accepts my reprogram of him, and that's the last we will ever hear of the idea. He will have given up by next year, and these companies rarely have printed materials.

A well-thought-out escape resolves a situation like this quickly, routinely, and almost on remote control. Standard answers for solicitors for charities work the same way. For example, since we give toothbrushes to our patients, people ask us to donate brushes to a church, school, or charitable cause.

Our office policy has already decided the issue. We will give two dozen toothbrushes to any legitimate group. The brush carries our name, so there is minimal advertising value, but it is extremely minimal. (Nobody chooses a dentist because the office name is on a toothbrush or on a refrigerator magnet.) Having predetermined decisions keeps these people from penetrating my conscious being, and I needn't reprogram them.

We give no free services—prophy, exam, or discount on a crown— to use in a charitable auction. We never give discount coupons, one of the worst marketing efforts imaginable. A discount is half a gift, worse than no gift. Discounts are like getting a new toy, without the batteries. Charitable contributions, solicited by credentialed people, all receive $5. Again, no input from me. Just do it.

We never allow an outside organization to solicit and sell anything within our office. The ban includes children and relatives of staff. I love Girl Scout cookies, but I do not want to be badgered or have the staff/team annoyed or pressured into buying anything on the job. I support the United Way as much as I know how, but we do not allow them or any other outside agencies to pitch staff for contributions.

We are a dental office—not a collection depot nor a retail outlet. We do not allow staff members to sell things to other staff members in the office or to set up home sales parties there. What they do outside the office is their business. Inside the office, what they do is my business. We don't allow smoking, either. Is there a difference?

Anyway, most people who want to reprogram us aren't really sure what they want. The bumper sticker on the car ahead of me screamed, "Recognize Laotia!" Gee, is there a Laotia? If I were to recognize it, what should I do? If I want to disregard it, what should I do? I'm confused about that request, but less so than the poor soul with the flaming bumper directive to nowhere.

The other day on the drive to work, a yard sign commanded me to "Keep the United States out of the United Nations!" You know what? I don't even know my own power. Trouble is, how shall I do it? Do you think I should get some reasons first, before I exercise my awesome puissance and take us out of the United Nations? Who said decisions in life are easy?

One license-plate frame really grabbed me by the throat. It commanded me to be an organ and tissue donor. I wanted to drive up to the car and ask the driver if I could finish with my parts before I had to donate them! He got away, so I guess I'll never know.

When I go to the chair, I say to my patient, "Hello, Betty. How are you?"

Betty wrings her hands, screws up her face, and mumbles in a sad cadence, "Oh, hello, doctor. I guess I'm as good as can be expected. How are you?"

Behind the chair my staff is having a silent hoot. They've heard me respond to this question a thousand times, and they know I am completely predictable.

"I'm Sooper, Betty!"

The office team got me a good one a few years ago. They gave me license plates for my car that announced a single word, which you have already guessed was "SOOPER."

What this says is that the dentist's attitude sets the pace in the dental office. Mary Kay Ash, founder of the Mary Kay Cosmetics Company in Dallas, Texas, has written, "The speed of the leader is the speed of the gang." Ask a Mary Kay representative (no, those on staff may not sell in the office!) if you may read her well-worn copy of Mary Kay's first book.

Not only does a super-day program work well for mental well-being, physical health—a proven fact—and practice profit, but being super in the office gears staff to work the same program. Since patients can detect a team rift the moment they enter the door, we help set the patient's program, as well. Patients pick up on staff happiness even faster.

Not one bad thing can come from programming our minds to have a superior day. On the contrary, an enormous number of good things can, and do, result from the right programs. Does this mean bad things don't happen to people programmed for super days?

Of course "stuff happens" to everyone. When negatives occur to programmed people, solutions come more quickly, the problem does not have lasting value, and the programmee returns to the kind of day he wanted to have, far more quickly. A bump in the road need not turn into a detour.

HAVE A FUN PRACTICE

Here's a question for you: What is fun? Isn't it interesting how differently we all interpret that little three-letter word, *fun*. As the trail through life gets longer, what adds to the interest is how much our personal definitions change. When we are introduced to a new hobby, a new sport, or a new friend, we alter our pleasure paths in minutes.

When I began my new practice, I had just come from a "sure thing" investment program. Let's make a point with that wall banger and move on.

With a failed mission statement crumpled up on the floor in St. Albans, I sold out and moved to Des Moines. In Iowa's biggest city, I worked with some recently-made friends on various business ventures. Our idea, in the beginning 1970s, was to buy companies in the health care industry, add up their profits, and—with a new stock issue—take the company public, multiplying the profits by factors of 10 or 20 to one.

Sounds good—too good. We bought some companies, had some nightmares, turned some businesses around, never quite found enough profits to add up for a new stock issue, and then two things happened. One, we ran out of seed money. No money, no businesses to buy. Two, the new-issues market dried up to nothing.

My fatal mistake was ego and me, I, and my. Without a shred of logic, I deduced that because I could play the pediatric dental game extremely well—and I had the bucks to prove it—I could deal myself into about any other business game I chose. It did not occur to me that the jackals with whom I had associated had spent their careers learning stealthy paths through jungles I didn't know existed.

I quickly learned I had established financial connections with wolves who had killed for lesser game. They courted me, pandered to my ego, and carefully performed an extraction from my wallet that was pure artistry. I should be so good at extracting a tooth.

A few years later, I left town far more wise and far more broke than I ever dreamed I could become. Both wisdom and financial failure were valuable lessons. There are two points I'd like to make by telling about this painful chapter of my life.

The lesson I learned is to invest only in a business I know as well as any of the other players, where I can either control the outcome or have liquidity, and where no other investor looks to me for a profit. The other point I'm not sure is learnable, but I think it can be learned. The point is *learn the lesson, then forget the learning.*

As I've been pounding this copy out on my laptop, I have tried to recall the names of the sharks who worked me over in Des Moines. For the life of me, I cannot remember a single name. That's because my mind cannot, or does not, remember bad stuff.

People tell me that failing to recall bad things is a blessing. I know it is, for when a team member makes an error, we learn from it—that is, I remonstrate with the employee, and we decide how to prevent the incident from recurring, then I put it completely out of my mind.

If this virtue is learnable, and I think maybe it is by using neuro-lingual programming (NLP), then it is a program with enough value to input into our brain-computer. More about NLP later, when I'll tell you how you can program some astonishing things with your mind.

I decided my new practice in Cedar Rapids would be a general practice. That decision came because, as I was going down the tubes in Des Moines, my friend Doug Johnson wheedled me into joining him for a day or two of practice weekly in nearby Newton, Iowa. Newton is famous for Fred Maytag having invented the bottom-agitator washing machine there, and pretty much erasing homemakers' blue Mondays.

Doug had a fine practice with Porter Wilson in a shopping center in Newton. After a couple of years out of dentistry, I wondered if I even knew which end of the handpiece to hold. Finally, I relented to his pleas and went to his chair as an associate.

My first patient was a tall senior and when he opened his mouth I thought I was looking into the Grand Canyon. Fourteen years of pedo can do that to a person. The space was cavernous. However, I soon began to enjoy adult patients almost as much as children. It did not take long to learn the rules which many generalists already appreciated.

As a pedodontist, I had always known half the answer, which was to treat three-year-olds like adults. It works. I always knelt down, shook their hands, looked them in the eye, and said, "Yes, a tiny, tiny bit!" when they asked if it was going to hurt. Children learn the H-word from parents, not dentists. Three-year-olds respond well to being treated like adults.

The adult equivalent was learned in Doug's practice. It is, to treat adults like three-year-olds. I have never had a dentist or a patient argue with that statement, so I know it's true.

In my new mission statement, I vowed to have fun with this practice. My definition of fun is as unique for me as yours is for you. I have fun when I have time to worship God. To have fun I must have quality time with my family, not sandwiched times. I cannot have fun unless I work with people who are joyful to be around, are sharp, have a good sense of humor, and are attractive (we'll get to that one in a minute).

My definition of fun means full chairs, a nice new patient flow, and a cash flow yielding some money at the end of my month, rather than some month at the end of my money. Fun means making a profit, providing quality dentistry, and getting most new referrals from existing patients.

Fun, in my book, is avoiding all the slams I've had into those hard dental walls and surviving those I cannot avoid. I don't think my definition is too demanding. I've had 20 years of it and it has been, well . . . it's been sooper.

Dissection Lab

Dentists recall that Anatomy 101 ended in the dissection lab where words on the pages became associated with real structures. The exercise gave the studies more relevance. Let's dissect the last chapter that began with embryology. We talked about:

- **Mission statements:** How to evaluate, build, and create a faulty mission statement, based solely on money.

- **After-hours emergency policy:** Never go to the office.

- **Sexual harassment:** Hold only three-party private meetings, or tape-record meetings and require a staff release.

- **Treat 3-year-olds like adults.**

- **Treat adults like 3-year-olds.**

- **The computer is like a brain.**

- **Program a sooper day:** Escape those who want to reprogram you and it's okay to fire some patients.

- **Investment parameters:** Invest in businesses you know as well as your competitors, where you control the outcome or have liquidity, and where no other investor looks to you for a profit.

- **A mission statement that works:** Have fun in dentistry.

- **Lobby for laws that prevent the disclosure of charges until they have been proven.**

- **Learn the lesson, then forget the learning.**

A ROSE IS A ROSE.

An employee is a teammate is a staff member is an assistant is a d.a. Which? Some people argue that we must always refer to staff members as *team* members. The apparent purpose is to instill *teamwork* in them. Really? I'm not sure that naming it a rose makes it a rose.

An associate once complained the staff didn't respect him enough. My response was that respect is an earned privilege. People render respect to others who they believe are entitled to respect. "You'll get it when you earn it, my friend," I told him.

So it is with being a team, being a teammate, and being a team member. Those titles reflect attitudes, but no matter what a person is called, if the office climate does not encourage, promote, and support teamwork, no title will change the facts.

When the office supports the team concept, members will know that truth, no matter what they are called.

CHAPTER TWO

OSTEOLOGY

"If the whole body were an eye,
where would the sense of hearing be? If the whole body
were an ear, where would the sense of smell be?
But, in fact, God has arranged the parts of the body,
every one of them, just as he wanted them to be.
If they were all one part, where would the body be?
As it is, there are many parts, but one body."

—1 CORINTHIANS, 12:17–20
THE NEW STUDY BIBLE, NIV
ZONDERVAN

Who is the most important person in the office? The question is a little bit like the preceding quote, and a little bit not. Each member of the office team—chairside assistants, hygienists, technicians, business staff, reception staff, doctors, and, yes, patients—has a right to answer the question of importance with, "Me!" Every one of them is right, of course, and a case can be made for each.

People won't appoint, as new patients, with unfriendly and belligerent receptionists. Collections won't occur when business receptionists fail to ask for payment. Office business affairs turn to shambles without a smart business staff. Statements unsent, appointments unconfirmed, business letters unmailed, and money unaccounted for wreak havoc on the rosiest of plans.

Hygiene production feeds the business with discovered work—like soil nutrients nourish plants—and paves the way for the doctor to keep open avenues of communication with the office menu of patients. Laboratory technicians provide products that are lookers and lasters, which become walking "billboards." Even the doctor often makes a useful contribution to the milieu.

Because the ultimate goal of the office is to deliver palatable dental services, the person who can influence that experience the most plays the key role in building practice longevity and future referrals. She is the chairside assistant, the dental assistant, the d.a.

The assistant controls the flow by keeping the doctor on time and preventing patients from waiting. She provides input to the doctor about special circumstances such as medical alerts, and she gives the doctor personal data about the patient to use as conversation starters.

The alert assistant updates the health history, goes over treatment plans, explains procedures and terms, makes financial plans, comforts the patient through the appointment, makes the return appointment, may collect payment, escorts the patient from the office, and makes patients feel important.

She's on the firing line, makes us look good or goofy, and she's worth a lot to the success of the office. The question is: How do we find, train, retain, and reward these valued teammates? Every time I think we have it figured out, the rules change. When we added in-house computers and dental management software, we lost two assistants, because they were unable to adapt to the new technology.

We taught expanded functions and ended up heavily fined for overstepping archaic rules. We began retirement programs and found they had little, if any, job retention power. We changed hours for workdays and found those hours didn't match earned vacation days. What do we do when a staff member wants a day (eight hours) of paid vacation but is working ten hours?

We took a dozen staffers to the ADA meeting in Hawaii, received front-page newspaper publicity (favorable) and then an IRS audit (unfavorable) came crashing down around us, costing tens of thousands of dollars. We got a time clock, then had the U.S. Commerce Department respond to a dissident staff complaint about not paying overtime. When it comes to staffing, one thing seems clear: Nothing is clear.

Contrary to the many speakers I have enjoyed hearing discourse on this topic, I don't have slick, packaged answers. Things change, so whatever I write next will be outdated much too soon, unless . . . unless I write conceptually and let specifics track the times, changing as needed.

Suggesting that you adapt what you are reading to the needs of your practice is a bit like telling my dog to shake when he gets out of the water. He's going to do it, anyway. Here are the concepts I've learned that enable the staff to remain a team.

ATTRACT ATTRACTIVE STAFF

How do we attract staff? With appealing want ads (Fig. 2–1). Most dental assistants in town look over the "dental assistant wanted" want ads every week or so. Why? Why not? Sharp people want to better themselves. That's the penalty that goes with hiring aggressive staff.

A dentist once complained to me that he was tired of applicants always harping about salary and benefits during employment interviews. I asked him how he thought an employee who doesn't care about her own income could possibly care about his?

Why should staff members care whether the office gets paid, without similar concerns for themselves? Over years of hiring hundreds of employees, I have learned that the staff members who want to work so badly they will work for almost anything—read that to mean almost nothing—are no bargain. My best and longest-term employees stated their salary and benefit requirements at the outset. I have paid them more and they have earned more for me. It's a wonderful trade.

Hire the applicants who have a goal and press for it. You'll pay pennies more and they'll make you dollars more. It's a great trade.

Your ad should identify your office. I have never understood the reason for secrecy, such as a blind box number. The ad tells the position available, the credentials required for the position—so long as they are not discriminatory and do not violate fair hiring practices. The ad tells when you want the person to begin work and lists your office telephone number. Put some pull in your ad. Have your want ad answer the question: Why should anyone, in her right mind, want to work in this office?

Times and markets change, too. Sometimes we have a surfeit of goodness, a dozen applicants, all with schooling. Sometimes we have but few inquiries, all from people seeking on-the-job training. These facts invite our team to be adaptable and do the best with what we get.

The interview process begins with the applicant's call to our office. The answering person makes notes of the person's name and telephone demeanor. These notations track the applicant through the process. This becomes the first interview, of sorts. Assuming the caller sounds fitting, she (most are women) is invited to come to the office to fill out an application (Fig. 2–2).

When she arrives at the office, the reception staff makes notes of how she presents herself, how she speaks, and how she deals with the receptionists. These are important observations.

The application is checked for obvious disqualifiers. For example, the applicant may note that she is unavailable after 5 P.M., she has not arranged for a sitter for her children, she is attending school or has another job and wants fill-in hours, all of which may be unacceptable to our staffing needs. References are called and the applicant's ability to match our wants is confirmed.

The applicant is invited for the screening interview with the office administrator. During this interview, our staff checks for reasons to disqualify the applicant. Almost all applicants *appear* to qualify, but many do not.

The trick is to discover the reasons we do not want to invest our time and money in this candidate. Money can easily be frittered away on people who should have been disbarred from the selection process long before they were hired. Our attitude stands steadfast: How can we keep this person out of our office, before we sink a few thousand dollars into training, and then find that we must send her packing?

Scores of firings later, we have learned a lot about who should and who should not receive serious consideration for a job opening. One reason, often missed, is overqualification. The scenario goes something like this.

Judy had a master's degree in English, was attractive, had an engaging personality, and desperately wanted to work for us.

"I've always wanted to work in the health care professions and when I saw your ad in the newspaper, well, I realized this was definitely me." We bought that line and hired Judy on the spot. Poor woman, there simply aren't many teaching jobs requiring master's degrees in English in our neck of the woods.

She was magnificent on the job. Learned at lightning speed, got along with staff and patients famously, blended into the team like she had been there years, instead of days.

Then the shoe hit the fan, or is it the other fan hit the floor? No matter. Judy came to us, real tears running down her cheeks.

"I hate to do this, but I must leave. I've been offered a position in translation for the local electronics firm. You see," we were spellbound by her story and could not tear ourselves away, "years ago, I participated in an exchange program with Tasmania and fell in love, and married this Tasmanian . . . shall we say, devil?" She let her little joke sink in.

"I learned, would you believe it?, the Tasmanian language, almost a lost tongue, and now, of all things, can you imagine, Rockwell Avionics needs a Tasmanian interpreter! I can't even guess how they heard about me." The fact that she had been sending resumés all over the area, of course, had nothing to do with this turn of events.

Lesson Number One: Do not hire people who are overqualified for the job. A job opening in their specialty will occur far sooner than you expect, and the time and money spent training will be wishes washed down the drain.

Sarah said it plainly, "We will never leave Cedar Rapids!"

The only trouble with that statement was that we believed it. We knew Sarah's husband was in management training for Slop Chute, a rapidly growing fast-food chain. She assured us over and over again that both of their families lived in our area, Slop Chute had seven local outlets, the company had promised them they would be in Cedar Rapids forever, and hell would freeze over before they would leave.

Guess what? Hell froze over. "Gee, I'm so sorry about Victor's promotion, but he's been offered the management of 13 Slop Chutes in

Kansas City." Sarah had the colossal gall to ask if I could help her get employment in Kansas City.

Ah shucks, you guessed it. We sent letters of inquiry to the largest dental offices in Kansas City for her, and helped her find a nice job. You never know. She might move back home.

Lesson Number Two: Check spouse job stability with a jaundiced eye. After you've sent enough of your job training funds to places like Kansas City, you will become a believer.

Brenda had passed screenings on the telephone, reception desk, and by the office administrator. Now she came to me for the final interview, the 60-second interview. It's the final piece in the employment puzzle. How can I interview someone in 60 seconds and tell if I want to hire him or her?

I can because it is the same way people interview us—or our staff, office, and people who act on our behalf on the telephone—in even less than 60 seconds. The impression that job applicants make on me, when they are on their best behavior, dressed in their Sunday-go-to-meetin' clothes, certainly tells me a lot about their first impressions on behalf of the office.

One of my first questions is about past bosses. "How is it going for ol' Jim Brown? Do they still let him practice?"

That question is a setup, of course. I have said something slightly derogatory about Jim, even though he's a good friend of mine, to test her reaction, to find out if she says something like, "Then you know about his dentistry?" or, "He was certainly not a very nice man."

If she agrees with me she may be lying, vindictive, or the reason she left Jim may be because of her problems, not his. Remotely, too, she might know something I don't. In any event, our interview is over. We will let her down nicely, "Thanks for coming in. We have promised four more interviews, and one seems to have had more experience than you."

Lesson Number Three: If she throws mud at a past employer, I look ahead six months and picture how she will trash me to someone else. No one needs this bad apple in the barrel.

If the 60-second interview works, my administrator—who has accompanied the aspirant to my office—knows I am agreeing to her employment when I launch into my "three people to please" speech.

THREE PEOPLE TO PLEASE

It goes like this: "You know, Kris, there are three people you must please to make this job work out, and I am not one of them." Kris does a little double take.

"You must please the patients. They pay all the freight. Without their happiness there is no job for you, or for me.

"Then you must get along with the rest of the staff. We have a team of experts working here who are professionals and do a professional job. You can be the greatest dental assistant in the world and you won't work here if you cannot get along with the world's finest dental staff, here at Gentle Dental.

"In that regard, may I say one more thing. You will see things happen here that are different than in any office you have ever worked in. Please remember that different does not mean inferior. Learn our way, thoroughly, by rote, first. Then if you have suggestions for improvement, make them to the office administrator, or to me. We have open minds, but please note we have a successful system that we will change only slowly and reluctantly.

"Finally, you must please yourself. When you go home at the end of a shift, I want you to feel good inside, knowing you have helped people, enriched their lives by affording them improved health, and that you have done so in a manner that gave them gentle experiences.

"If you have pleased the patient, become a part of the team, and satisfied yourself, there is no way on earth that you could fail to please me."

I ask Kris if she truly wants to work in our office, having just received a tour prior to the 60-second interview. When she vows that nothing would be finer, I ask her and the office administrator to see if they can work out terms of employment. The application has already asked her what starting salary would be necessary to obtain her employment, and when she could begin, so I can see whether or not we have common ground.

Sometimes people have higher hopes than our payment schedule permits. We then must either yield, and pay the asking price, or negotiate. "Let's start you at our starting wage, and if you learn as quickly as we think you will, and if you show us you are as good as we think you are, you will be at your requested wage in no time."

The negotiation usually works because applicants often give themselves a raise when they put down their starting requirements. Sometimes we misjudge, and an applicant finds another office that will pay the desired wage. The best way to counter this—if you really want this person—is to follow your applicant closely. Call the applicant that evening, for example, if he or she did not accept your first job offer. If the office acts quickly enough, and has made a good enough impression, a quick counteroffer can be made on the phone to salvage the employment.

Good employees should earn the office three times their salary. One-third goes for overhead, one-third for salary, and one-third for office profit. That's an old rule that many corporations have used effectively for years. Applied to the employment of an associate, a hygienist, or any other staff member, the formula is about the same. Some jobs, however, since they are not for primary providers, make it difficult to correlate production against costs.

Two Winning Attributes

We watch closely for two key elements in job applicants—personality and appearance. We can teach dentistry. Personality must be original equipment. Given a certified dental assistant with six years of experience (in an office comparable to ours) and possessing a dishrag personality, weighed against an applicant who needs training, but has a bubbly personality, I'll hire smiles every time.

Why? I know, it is a strange question, but there are doctors who have asked it. Because the dental experience is about all we have to sell. Oh, we both know that many believe we sell crowns, bridges, fillings, extractions, sealants, and prophys. Those who believe that don't understand what people buy and why. We will cover those elements later.

The lady with personality will make patients feel good. There is precious little in this profession that makes people feel good. If you find someone who has that ability, cashing in on her personality is money in your bank.

Appearance is the other half of the chief requirements for staff. This does not mean staff must be runway-fashion models. We want people who are pleasant and whom we *think* are attractive.

Haven't you met scores of people throughout life who certainly could not model for magazines but whom you genuinely thought were pretty? They could be pounds overweight, maybe not have the most dashing hairdo, perhaps be dressed in dowdy clothing, but they had a presence, an attraction, an aura that made people want to be with them.

Attractiveness is an invaluable intangible smart employers trade on daily. Dr. Ellen Berscheid, of the University of Minnesota, conducted a study of the comely and came to some amazing conclusions. She reported that attractive people of our society constitute a privileged class. In what she calls a "strong, physical attractiveness stereotype," Dr. Berscheid has found that attractive people are assumed to be "kinder, more genuine, sincere, warm, sexually responsive, poised, modest, sociable, sensitive, interesting, strong, more exciting, more nurturant, and of better character than the less handsomely endowed."

Given the competitiveness of today's dental scene, does it make sense for us to staff our offices with people who do not bring those attributes to work with them every day?

BRINGING STAFF ON LINE

Once the staff member is hired, a sequence of events occurs, as noted in a checkoff list on the application. These events are carved in stone. We may not skip one of them, and they must be done in order. The previous application lists them.

All new employees are hired conditionally (Fig. 2–3). The normal trial period is three months. The statement notes that this short period of time does not qualify for unemployment benefits.

Attention is called to the fact that the employee may terminate this agreement at any time, without prejudice and without offering an excuse.

We explain to new employees that we are giving them the right to walk off the job at 10 A.M. on Wednesday morning, no excuses needed, asked, or required, and no employment black mark. We explain that sometimes jobs just don't work out. We understand that, and we are willing to give them the freedom to accept or reject our office style. New employees feel comfortable with this escape clause.

A pendulum swings back and forth, so here's the kicker. By the same token, we point out, when we give this right we also retain the same right. That is, if we decide at 3 P.M. Thursday that the job isn't working out for the new employee, we will cancel her computer security, ask her to punch out, and pay her to that moment. There will be no questions asked, no excuses given, no questions answered. Simple, straightforward, upfront, and a back door—all important attributes of credible employment.

What prompts such an attitude? Have an irate husband camp on your doorstep when you discharge his wife after the first few days, and you will quickly understand the immense intelligence behind these measures. It only takes one, the one you needn't ever have.

Another provision of the conditional employment agreement is that free dental care must be paid for if employment does not continue for a full year. This provision came from employees joining the team, receiving large amounts of free dental care, then leaving. A slick deal if you can get it, but not in our office. Health insurance premiums are prorated the same way.

The initial agreement states that the new employee has been taught infection barrier control. This item is useful for OSHA requirements. The employee agrees to abide by office policies. She agrees to conduct herself in a professional manner on and off the job. Did we really want a go-go dancer by night, known as an assistant in our office? Did we really want a staffer on duty who couldn't talk without profanity? I think not.

She authorizes a reference check and agrees that our maternity leave and jury duty policies are acceptable. During the past 18 years, more than 40 staff members have gone through pregnancy while employed in our office. Several have worked chairside until 5 P.M. and delivered the baby that night.

The staff does all the expected baby shower things and conducts a lottery on date of delivery, size, and sex of the newborn. We have a lot of fun with babies and we have had a lot of experience. The staff member selects how long she wishes to be off for maternity leave. Some want as few as three weeks, some want six weeks or longer. We just want our newcomer to understand we think babies are wonderful and have all you want.

When staff members are subpoenaed for jury duty, we send a letter to the court and ask to have them dismissed. We have always received fine court cooperation, but we want the staffer to understand we will ask for their dismissal due to employment in a health care field.

All office statements are notarized by a staff member who is a notary public. To become a notary, the cost is low, the requirements are easy to fulfill, and the convenience of having a staff member able to notarize signatures in the office is equal to the ability to fax documents in the office. Running a business without either is inconceivable in these times.

Another document the new employee must sign is the *Biohazard Waste Acknowledgment Agreement* (Fig. 2–4). This covers our OSHA tracks and indicates the new staffer has been schooled in the proper handling and disposal of hazardous waste, understands the definitions of biohazardous, and acknowledges the appropriate defense attire and safety measures.

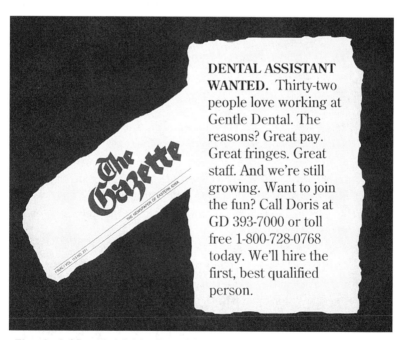

Fig. 2–1 Classified Ad for Dental Assistant.

$\mathbb{G}$entle $\mathbb{D}$ental

CONFIDENTIAL APPLICATION FOR EMPLOYMENT

Name _____ tele. # _____ date _____

Address _____ how long?_____

Previous address _____ how long?_____

Social Security # _____

number of children _____ ages _____

_____ due to federal law the answers to these questions _____
are voluntary and not required for employment

Date of birth _____ Place_____

Height_____ Weight _____ Race _____ Sex ☐ M   ☐ F

Marital status (check one) ☐ S   ☐ M   ☐ D   ☐ W   ☐ SEP

Spouse's name_____

Employment _____

Do you have any hour limitations for working? _____

Do you have any health problems? _____

Condition of health? _____

 Whom should we notify in case of an emergency?_____

Their phone # _____ Their relationship _____

List past employers, starting with the most recent. Indicate for each: 1. name and location of employer, 2. dates of employment, 3. your position and duties, 4. your salary, 5. what you enjoyed most about that job, and 6. what you enjoyed least; why you left that employment?

1._____

2._____

3._____

4._____

5._____

6._____

Fig. 2–2 Confidential application for employment.

1. _____
2. _____
3. _____
4. _____
5. _____
6. _____

1. _____
2. _____
3. _____
4. _____
5. _____
6. _____

PLEASE TELL US ABOUT YOUR EDUCATION

Your highest level of schooling ☐ 12 ☐ 13 ☐ 14 ☐ 15 ☐ 16+
Degrees? _____
Certification? ☐ RDH   ☐ CDT   ☐ CDA   ☐ CPR   ☐ X-ray

PLEASE TELL US ABOUT YOUR HEALTH

Are you hepatitis vaccinated?_____ Pregnant?_____
Have you ever had?   ☐ heart disease   ☐ diabetes   ☐ hepatitis
☐ AIDS/HIV antibodies   ☐ rheumatic fever   ☐ asthma   ☐ epilepsy
☐ psychological or psychiatric treatment   ☐ high b/p

PLEASE TELL US ABOUT YOU

Have you ever had trouble with the law or with drugs? _____
What are your six best assets?
1. _____ 4. _____
2. _____ 5. _____
3. _____ 6. _____
Are you confident? _____
How do you see yourself? _____
Why do you feel you are suited for this position? _____
What salary would it require to obtain your employment? _____
How soon would you be willing to begin? _____

Fig. 2–2 *(Continued)*

I authorize all schools, credit bureaus, former employers, and law enforcement agencies to supply information about my background to Gentle Dental East. I understand that if any statement is later found to be untrue, offers of employment may be withdrawn, or I may be dismissed, without compensation.

Signed _____Date _____

FOR OFFICE USE ONLY

1. Application filled out
2. Tour
3. References Called
4. Time Card
5. Determine Salary and Starting Date
6. Employee Manuals Read and Explained, Copy given
7. Badge
8. Heptavax if in Category I or II
9. OSHA Film
10. OSHA Training
11. OSHA Manual
12. Computer Security
13. Enter in Security File
14. Enter in Seniority File
15. Enter in Staff Address File
16. X-ray Certificate
17. Computer Training
18. Insurance Training
19. Sterilization Training
20. Welcome to GDE staff notice
21. Treatment of HIV/AIDS Patients
22. Employment Release Form
23. CPR Certificate—new or renewal

Fig. 2–2 *(Continued)*

CONDITIONAL EMPLOYMENT AGREEMENT

My signature below acknowledges my assent.

I understand that I am employed for a trial period of (weeks/months). I understand this does not constitute full-time employment, qualifying for unemployment benefits.

During this trial period either GD or I may terminate this agreement, without prejudice. I do not have to tell GD my reason for departure, just as GD does not have to tell me the reason for my dismissal.

Dental Care Agreement

If free dental care has been given to me and my family during my employment at GD, it was given to me with the understanding that I would remain an employee of GD for at least one year.

If my employment terminates—for whatever reason—prior to one year, I agree to repay GD for the portion of dental work that was a gift to me and members of my family. This amount will be deducted from the last paycheck.

Infection Barrier Control

I have been taught infection control, how to handle hazardous chemicals in normal usage, in disposal, and during abnormal incidents. I have been taught cross-contamination control and how to handle biohazardous materials and how to deal with abnormal incidents.

My instructions have been in accord with the CDC, ADA, and OSHA requirements and recommendations. I have reviewed the "Infection Control" video and understand the special hazards peculiar to my position at GD.

In consideration of my employment, I agree to conform to the rules and standards of this office as they may from time to time be amended.

I agree to conduct myself in an appropriate professional manner at all times, both within and outside of the office, and that failure to do so, as judged by the management of GD, may be cause for dismissal.

Fig. 2–3 Conditional employment agreement.

I authorize the references listed by me on my application for employment, and all other individuals whom you may contact, to provide any and all information concerning my prior employment. I release all parties and persons from any and all liability that may result.

I understand that the policies of GD allow me appropriate maternity leave, as may be required, without penalty. I understand that I may have time off for jury duty, if required, but that normal practice at GD is to apply for dismissal from jury duty, which usually is granted.

I agree that my trial employment can be terminated at will, with or without cause, with or without notice, at any time, at either my option or at the option of GD.

Signed _____ Date_____

Witnessed _____ Date_____

Fig. 2–3 *(Continued)*

The new employee also signs a statement of knowledge (Fig. 2–5), announcing she has been trained in and agrees to certain office protocols. She admits to being instructed in OSHA policies, rules, and regulations, and that she has observed the ADA instructional video.

She admits her understanding that fraudulent billing practices and failure to report income for tax purposes are forbidden at Gentle Dental.

She accepts the fact that prescription drugs may not be given to staff for any nondental reason, that dental assistants will be trained, instructed in, and allowed to perform only legally approved duties, and that sexual harassment is forbidden. She makes these statements of her own free will and then comes the final agreement:

> I further agree that if any dispute about the terms of my employment, my performance on the job, any claim of harassment, discrimination, or any other claim whatsoever shall arise, during or following my

employment, it shall be submitted to arbitration under Chapter 679A of the Code of Iowa (1993). It is understood by both myself and Gentle Dental that by agreeing to submit all claims or assertions that either Gentle Dental or I may have against the other arising out of this agreement, Gentle Dental and I have given up our right to a jury or a court trial.

You have just read the most powerful statement that has ever appeared in print concerning legal aspects of dentistry. I repeat the disclaimer that appeared in the front of this book: Every state has a different set of laws. What may work in one state may not in another. As a matter of fact, this law has not yet been tested in Iowa. Implement no policy or document that has legal ramifications until you have received your attorney's blessing.

GIVING UP A RIGHT TO SUE

How did we happen on this approach? My trusted attorney and I have a fine relation. He helped me set up a revocable living trust (RLT). Many people should consider setting up the RLT for its several aspects. Those benefits include: Privacy (the estate value is not published), speed (probate takes far longer to close an estate), and cost (attorney's fees are substantially less to close an estate that flows to heirs through the living trust).

One day after work, I met with my attorney for a libation and chat. He was a bit down, explaining that his firm had incurred a large settlement for a professional liability exposure. I asked what would happen to their insurance premiums and he answered that the firm had taken steps to assuage future losses.

What were those steps? There were several things the firm was going to do, including buying a large deductible policy, but one feature stood out. From now on, the firm's clients must agree to binding arbitration if there is any dispute over fee or representation.

Dead silence. I couldn't believe my ears. My immediate question: Is it legal for people to give up their right to sue?

BIOHAZARD WASTE ACKNOWLEDGMENT AGREEMENT

I, the undersigned, understand the following information on the OSHA regulations concerning the proper handling and disposal of biohazardous waste:

The following items (and their like) are considered biohazardous waste and materials:

When used on or in presence of patient: Gloves, Clinic Jackets, Eyewear, Masks, and Face Shields.

When used on patient, or if these items have contacted Saliva, Blood, or Blood products of patient: Bibs, Gauze, Cotton Rolls, Tissues, Other paper products, Disposable instruments, Prophy angles, Cotton Tips, and other such items.

These items are biohazardous: Saliva, Blood, Tissue, Teeth, Blood products, Any and ALL items contacted with, containing, or soaked with Saliva, Blood and Blood products.

The proper way to dispose of these items: In ANY receptacle labeled with the orange BIOHAZARD sticker.

Except for clinic jackets which are placed in a BIOHAZARD labeled laundry bag at the end of the day, or immediately if they have become soaked with biohazardous materials.

Any item that is not considered biohazardous waste must be thrown away in a container WITHOUT the orange BIOHAZARD sticker.

At NO time may biohazardous waste be disposed of in a container not labeled as biohazard. This is in direct violation of OSHA regulation and could result in a citation or fine to this office.

It is the responsibility of this office to ensure ALL employees of this office (which includes everyone working in this building) follow the guidelines set by OSHA and IOSHA (Iowa Occupational Safety and Health Administration). Under no circumstances is anyone exempt from these rules.

I, the undersigned, have read the above and I understand what biohazardous waste is, and how to handle and dispose of the waste properly. All my questions have been answered concerning biohazardous waste.

Signature _____ Date _____

Fig. 2–4 Biohazard waste acknowledgment agreement.

NEW TEAM MEMBER'S STATEMENT OF KNOWLEDGE

OSHA

I understand that I will be instructed in OSHA policies, rules, and regulations and by reading required and appropriate materials, and by observing the American Dental Association OSHA video.

Financial

I understand that fraudulent billing practices and failure to report income for tax purposes are forbidden at GD.

Prescription Drugs

I understand that no drugs can be prescribed for employees, except for dental reasons.

Dental Assistant Duties

I understand that I will be trained in the duties that are allowed to be legally performed by those in my position.

Sexual Harassment

I understand the Gentle Dental office policy forbidding sexual harassment and agree not to violate this rule.

My Statement of Free Will

I make these statements of my own free will. I have not been coerced or forced to make them under any threat. I will report all violations of any of these rules at once to the office administrator. I may report violations to any appropriate state or federal agency.

I further agree that if any dispute about the terms of my employment, my performance on the job, any claim of harassment, discrimination, or any other claim whatsoever shall arise, during or following my employment, it shall be submitted to arbitration under Chapter 679A of the Code of Iowa (1993). It is understood by both myself and Gentle Dental that by agreeing to submit all claims or assertions that either Gentle Dental or I may have against the other, arising out of this agreement, Gentle Dental and I have given up our right to a jury or a court trial.

Signed_____ Dated _____

Witnessed _____ Dated _____

Subscribed and sworn to me this _____ Day of _____, 1995.

_____

Jean M. Corey, Notary Public

Fig. 2–5 New team member's statement of knowledge.

Fig. 2–6 Schmidty's dental team, circa 1995, Cancun, Mexico: The happy winners!

The answer: Yes, we do it all the time, with certain insurance, bank, and stockbroker transactions. Suddenly the light went on. If a legal firm could reduce its liability exposure by having clients agree to arbitration, why could a dental office not do the same thing?

No reason why not, except that there were no case precedents about the concept. It hadn't appeared in court to test its validity. No matter. I immediately incorporated the concept in all patient registrations for new patients, all informed consents, and all staff disclaimers.

Will it hold in court? I have no idea. Time will tell. Again, I make no claim for this approach. I do not know how this kind of document might work in your state. Nor do I know if your professional liability insurance company would even permit their client dentists to collect such documents.

To date, no patient has refused to sign the document. Of course, people with litigious intent usually get that way after the fact, not before. Since we began this policy, several inquiries have been received from law firms about patients we have treated. These were answered with copies of the arbitration agreement and we have not heard from them again. I do not know if the document deterred any planned action. We will continue asking for signatures.

Each quarter, we ask all staff to sign a document called the *Team Member's Statement of Knowledge* (Fig. 2–8). This document states the staff member: has been properly instructed in OSHA and knows of no violations, knows of no improper coding and fraudulent billing, and knows of no funds that were unreported for tax purposes.

The statement goes on to aver that the signer knows of no prescriptions that were written for illegal purposes, has not known dental assistants to have performed, or been asked to perform, illegal duties.

The statement concludes with the undersigned agreeing that no instance of sexual harassment has occurred at GD, and that the staff member agrees to binding arbitration, in the event of any past or future dispute. All assistants, hygienists, and doctors sign the statement, which is notarized by another staff member who conveniently is a notary public.

New staff members also sign *Form ED-3* (Fig. 2–9), an exposure determination record; *Form VA-1* (Fig. 2–10), a vaccination record, and an acknowledgment that they have reviewed the OSHA tapes (Fig. 2–11). One more document states that they understand the GD office policy on treating the HIV+ or AIDS patient (Fig. 2–12). They sign their *W-4* forms (Fig. 2–13), the *Department of Justice Employment Eligibility Verification* forms (Fig. 2–7) and the *State Employee's Withholding Allowance Certificates* (Fig. 2–14).

The new employee entrance protocol requires the employee to read and understand the *Employee Manual,* which is a job description, a mission manual, and an explanation of acceptable conduct for GD staff (Appendix C). Though the manuals are job-specific for doctors, hygienists, business/receptionists, and chairside assistants, certain data is the same for all.

New staffers must view OSHA tapes and undergo OSHA training. X-ray certification or registration, if appropriate for the position, is begun. Computer training commences, and for chairside assistants, the move toward the operatory begins with a stint working with the rovers to learn infection barrier techniques at GD.

U.S. Department of Justice
Immigration and Naturalization Service

OMB No. 1115-0136
Employment Eligibility Verification

Please read instructions carefully before completing this form. The instructions must be available during completion of this form. ANTI-DISCRIMINATION NOTICE. It is illegal to discriminate against work eligible individuals. Employers CANNOT specify which document(s) they will accept from an employee. The refusal to hire an individual because of a future expiration date may also constitute illegal discrimination.

Section 1. Employee Information and Verification. To be completed and signed by employee at the time employment begins

Print Name: Last	First	Middle Initial	Maiden Name

Address (Street Name and Number)	Apt. #	Date of Birth (month/day/year)

City	State	Zip Code	Social Security #

I am aware that federal law provides for imprisonment and/or fines for false statements or use of false documents in connection with the completion of this form.

I attest, under penalty of perjury, that I am (check one of the following):
☐ A citizen or national of the United States
☐ A Lawful Permanent Resident (Alien # A____)
☐ An alien authorized to work until ____/____/____
(Alien # or Admission # ____)

Employee's Signature

Date (month/day/year)

Preparer and/or Translator Certification. (To be completed and signed if Section 1 is prepared by a person other than the employee.) I attest, under penalty of perjury, that I have assisted in the completion of this form and that to the best of my knowledge the information is true and correct.

Preparer's/Translator's Signature	Print Name

Address (Street Name and Number, City, State, Zip Code)	Date (month/day/year)

Section 2. Employer Review and Verification. To be completed and signed by employer. Examine one document from List A OR examine one document from List B and one from List C as listed on the reverse of this form and record the title, number and expiration date, if any, of the document(s)

List A	OR	List B	AND	List C
Document title:				
Issuing authority:				
Document #:				
Expiration Date (if any): ___/___/___		___/___		___/___/___
Document #:				
Expiration Date (if any): ___/___/___				

CERTIFICATION - I attest, under penalty of perjury, that I have examined the document(s) presented by the above-named employee, that the above-listed document(s) appear to be genuine and to relate to the employee named, that the employee began employment on (month/day/year) ___/___/___ and that to the best of my knowledge the employee is eligible to work in the United States. (State employment agencies may omit the date the employee began employment).

Signature of Employer or Authorized Representative	Print Name	Title

Business or Organization Name	Address (Street Name and Number, City, State, Zip Code)	Date (month/day/year)

Section 3. Updating and Reverification. To be completed and signed by employer

A. New Name (if applicable)	B. Date of rehire (month/day/year) (if applicable)

C. If employee's previous grant of work authorization has expired, provide the information below for the document that establishes current employment eligibility.

Document Title: _____ Document #: _____ Expiration Date (if any): ___/___/___

I attest, under penalty of perjury, that to the best of my knowledge, this employee is eligible to work in the United States, and if the employee presented document(s), the document(s) I have examined appear to be genuine and to relate to the individual.

Signature of Employer or Authorized Representative	Date (month/day/year)

Form I-9 (Rev. 11-21-91) N

Fig. 2–7 Department of Justice employment eligibility verification.

TEAM MEMBER'S STATEMENT OF KNOWLEDGE

OSHA

I have been instructed in OSHA policies, rules, regulations, and practices by being personally taught by the office Exposure Control Manager, who is a trained staff member, by reading required and appropriate materials, and by observing the American Dental Association OSHA video. I understand these materials and state that I know of no violation of OSHA rules, currently or in the past year, at Gentle Dental.

Financial

I know of no instance where any doctor or employee at Gentle Dental has charted any circumstance that did not occur exactly as charted. I know of no fraudulent billing of a patient, an insurer, or Title XIX. I know of no funds received in this office that have not been reported for tax purposes.

Prescription Drugs

I know of no instance where drugs have been prescribed for nondental needs either for patients or for staff members at Gentle Dental. I know of no instance of drug abuse either by staff members or doctors at Gentle Dental.

Dental Assistant Duties

I am trained in the duties that are allowed to be legally performed by a dental assistant (or by a dental hygienist, if appropriate) and state that I have not performed any illegal duties. I have not been asked to perform illegal duties and I have seen neither other dental assistants nor hygienists perform duties that are not allowed under the license laws of Iowa. I have not known of anyone at Gentle Dental asking an assistant or hygienist to perform an illegal duty.

Sexual Harassment

I understand the Gentle Dental office policy forbidding sexual harassment in the workplace and state that I have never seen, heard, or known of a single instance of sexual harassment occurring at Gentle Dental either by staff or by doctors.

My Statement of Free Will

While I have been asked to make this statement by the staff of Gentle Dental, I state that I make these statements of my own free will. I have not been coerced

Fig. 2–8 Quarterly staff statement of knowledge.

or forced to make them under the threat of losing my job or reducing my salary or hours.

I further understand that I have been informed that I may report future violations of any of the above circumstances to various state and local agencies.

I further agree that if any dispute about the terms of my employment, my performance on the job, any claim of harassment, discrimination, or any other claim whatsoever shall arise, during or following my employment, it shall be submitted to arbitration under Chapter 679A of the Code of Iowa (1993). It is understood by both myself and Gentle Dental that by agreeing to submit all claims or assertions that either Gentle Dental or I may have against the other, arising out of this agreement, Gentle Dental and I have given up our right to a jury or a court trial.

Signed _____ Dated _____

Witnessed _____ Dated _____

Subscribed and sworn to me this _____ Day of _____, 1995.

_____
Jean M. Corey, Notary Public

© 1995, Success Press

Fig. 2–8 *(Continued)*

WE ARE ALL ALIKE

If you view this schedule to be onerous, complex, and perhaps overkill, consider that every dental office is imperiled by the same potential exposures. Biohazards in my office are exactly the same as in your office. The same is true with federal laws, basic dental practice acts, and the risk of litigation, both from employees and from patients. If GD employed four people, I would not change one whit of this entrance protocol.

We may subspecialize in different aspects of dentistry, refer different problems to specialists, vary our crown preparation techniques,

FORM ED-3 — EXPOSURE DETERMINATION RECORD

As required by the OSHA Bloodborne Standard, the designated employee was classified according to job classifications, tasks, and procedures that expose such employee to infectious materials on (date)_____ as follows:

EMPLOYEE name_____ SS# _____
Job Title _____

☐ Category 1: "Job classifications in which ALL employees are exposed" to potentially infectious materials.
☐ Category 2: "Job classifications in which SOME employees are exposed" to potentially infectious materials.

EMPLOYEE signature _____
EMPLOYER signature _____

Because of a change of job assignment, the above employee was reclassified according to task exposure on (date) _____ as follows:
☐ Category 1
☐ Category 2

EMPLOYEE signature _____
EMPLOYER signature _____

Because of a change of job assignment, the above employee was reclassified according to task exposure on (date) _____ as follows:
☐ Category 1
☐ Category 2

EMPLOYEE signature _____
EMPLOYER signature _____

NOTE: This record should be retained for length of employment plus 30 years.
(FORM ED-3)

Fig. 2–9 ED-3 (exposure determination record).

FORM VA-1 VACCINATION RECORD

The following employee has received required training and, within 10 working days of initial assignment, was offered a test for hepatitis B according to recommendations of the U.S. Public Health Service on (date) _____

Employee name _____ SS#_____

Job Title of employee _____

1. ☐ Accepted
2. ☐ Declined (Understanding of statement below is acknowledged)

"I understand that due to my occupational exposure to blood or other potentially infectious materials I may be a risk of acquiring hepatitis B virus (HBV) infection. I have been given the opportunity to be vaccinated with hepatitis B vaccine, at no charge to myself. However, I decline hepatitis B vaccination at this time. I understand that by declining this vaccine, I continue to be at risk of acquiring hepatitis B, a serious disease. If in the future I continue to have occupational exposure to blood or other potentially infectious materials and I want to be vaccinated with hepatitis B vaccine, I can receive the vaccination series at no charge to me."

     Employee signature _____

3. ☐ Not Needed (Written proof of immunity has been provided for my record)

     Employee signature _____

Results of testing and/or vaccination _____

_____

_____

☐ The employee received a booster of hepatitis B according to recommendations of the U.S. Public Health Service on (date)_____

     Employee signature _____

Signature of Employer _____ Date _____

NOTE: This record should be retained for length of employment plus 30 years.

(FORM VA-1)

Fig. 2–10 VA-1 (vaccination record).

OSHA TAPES

I have viewed the following required OSHA tapes:

Infection Control in the Dental Environment
Principles and Fundamentals of Infection Control

Infection Control in the Dental Environment
Clinical Procedures

Infection Control in the Dental Environment
Sterilization and Disinfection

_____ Date_____

(c) 1995, Success Press

Fig. 2–11 OSHA tape review.

and offer different services to our patients, but a crown margin in your office is the same as in mine.

Similarly, a patient lawsuit, dissident employee legal action, Board of Dental Examiners penalty, or investment loss may be just as disastrous for you as for me. Dental office size has nothing to do with quality dental care, in either of our offices, and bigness or smallness does not excuse failure to deal appropriately with anyone, patient or staff member.

During our discussion of computers in the dental office, in a subsequent chapter, I will point out that the same advice holds true. Your computer must perform exactly as mine.

PUTTING IT TOGETHER

How do we assemble these documents? Start with a checklist and take it one page at a time. Mentally walk a new employee through the steps required to become a protected, knowledgable, useful staff member. Borrow patterns or paragraphs from illustrations in this book. Ask management consultants. Read other management texts from PennWell's extraordinary list of books.

Ask staff to help, then pay them for the effort. Assign different duties to the team and bring them together in staff meetings to discuss the real objective of putting the office down on paper.

Why is this exercise so crucial to office success? Airplane pilots never take off without going through a printed checklist. The reason is obvious. In the same manner, a practice will never take off without a checklist.

Second, the exercise of putting the office operational plan down on paper will help the team discover omissions, errors, and lost emphasis. Our focus can blur when the subject is a mental image, rather than a printed page. Unless you can see your goal clearly, you will never realize it.

A couple of years ago, I faced the challenge of deciding whether to retire or expand. I had mulled on that decision for some time, vacillating between retirement, as most of my colleagues had chosen, or going for one last hurrah.

My practice was in fine shape, with 11 chairs, three doctors, three hygienists, an excellent new patient flow of several hundred new patients each month, good market position, and stable cash flow. I could walk away and my daughter Catherine, a hygienist in the office, could manage the day-to-day duties and I could play the role of rainmaker. (A rainmaker is a retired lawyer who brings clients to the office whom his colleagues serve.)

As I stewed over the decision, a realtor called and asked if my office was for sale. A believer in omens, I immediately said yes, and in a few weeks my office building sold. Possession was to occur the following April, so there was time to build a new office in a rapidly growing section of town, near malls, new homes, and an interstate highway.

As I studied potential sites, I chanced on an 8,000-square-foot, empty office building in the heart of my target area. When I walked through the building, I failed to see how my practice would fit in this monstrosity. The next day I returned and suddenly saw my goal.

My new office jumped clearly into my mind, just as it appears today. Until I could see it, however, it could never become reality. Until we can see our future in our mind's eye, it remains an unfulfilled fantasy.

HOW TO TREAT THE HIV+ OR AIDS PATIENT AT GENTLE DENTAL

November, 1994

HIV: Human Immunodeficiency Virus

AIDS: Acquired Immune Deficiency Syndrome

When we learn that a patient is HIV positive (or HIV+ with the signs of AIDS), here is the law about what happens next:

1. Seat the patient.

It is illegal to refuse treatment of patients due to HIV. Upon learning of the patient's HIV+ status, the receptionist will immediately consult the dentist. The dentist will examine the patient and coordinate ALL treatment.

2. Treat the patient.

No assistant can be forced to work on an HIV+ patient. However, if you are willing to help a doctor or a hygienist treat an AIDS patient, please tell the Office Administrator.

By law, neither a dentist nor a hygienist may refuse to treat an AIDS patient. The penalty can be thousands of dollars and is the responsibility of the dentist or hygienist who refuses treatment. Gentle Dental, p.c., will not pay legal defense, fines, or penalties if a staff member of GD is fined for noncompliance with the law.

If the dentist is unable to obtain assistance, the dentist will refer the patient to U of I, College of Dentistry AIDS Treatment Center, offering this explanation:

"I am willing to treat you but, since I do not have an assistant who is willing to help me and, since I cannot force any assistant to help me work for an HIV+ patient, the things I can do for you are limited. They are limited because the standard of care in Iowa requires me to perform almost every procedure with an assistant.

"My inability to treat you is *unrelated* to your HIV status. (Make this perfectly clear!) The UI College of Dentistry has a staff able to perform every dental procedure and they see HIV+ patients the day they call for an appointment. After I examine your needs, our staff will be happy to call the college and help you arrange an immediate appointment."

University of Iowa, College of Dentistry: (319) 335-7447 (walk-ins accepted, call first)

Fig. 2–12 How to treat the HIV+ or AIDS patient at Gentle Dental.

3. Keep our mouths shut.

Patient confidentiality is required for every Gentle Dental patient. You may tell **only** the treating doctor when you learn of an HIV+ patient status. The doctor can **only** visit with staff members who will treat the patient. An HIV+ status can **never** be a topic of office gossip. You **may not** tell anyone outside the office about having seen an HIV+ or AIDS patient at GD. That restriction includes your closest family members.

What does it matter if you tell someone about a patient's HIV+ status? As soon as your leak becomes known, here's what will happen: The patient will sue you; you will make the front page of the *Gazette;* you will go to court; you will have to hire an expensive attorney; you will be found guilty; you will be fined thousands of dollars that will come out of your pocket; you may spend time in prison; you will be disgraced; and you will lose your job.

Did we dream up those penalties? Not for a minute. These dire results have happened already to other people in the United States. We didn't make it up. You have been fairly warned.

Remember "Universal Precautions":

No special sterilizing techniques are required to treat an HIV+ patient at Gentle Dental. The reason? We already use Universal Precautions (UP.) Today and every day, each and every patient is treated as though they were HIV+ or Hepatitis B positive. If you wish still more protection, GD has disposable caps, face shields, face masks, and sleeves and full gowns available.

A caller or a patient asks:

"Do you treat AIDS patients at Gentle Dental?"

Both federal and state law make it illegal to refuse to treat any patient. Have we treated any AIDS patients? We are forbidden to discuss any patient without their permission. A smart move is to refer the questioner to Dr. Schmidt.

I have read this Gentle Dental HIV/AIDS policy and agree to abide by all requirements that affect my position at GD. I will report all violations of this policy at once to Dr. Schmidt the senior dentist on duty.

Signature _____ Date _____

Witnessed_____ Date _____

Fig. 2–12 (*Continued*)

Form W-4 (1995)

Want More Money In Your Paycheck? If you expect to be able to take the earned income credit for 1995 and a child lives with you, you may be able to have part of the credit added to your take-home pay. For details, get Form W-5 from your employer.

Purpose. Complete Form W-4 so that your employer can withhold the correct amount of Federal income tax from your pay.

Exemption From Withholding. Read line 7 of the certificate below to see if you can claim exempt status. *If exempt, complete line 7; but do not complete lines 5 and 6.* No Federal income tax will be withheld from your pay. Your exemption is good for 1 year only. It expires February 15, 1996.

Note: *You cannot claim exemption from withholding if (1) your income exceeds $650 and includes unearned income (e.g., interest and dividends) and (2) another person can claim you as a dependent on their tax return.*

Basic Instructions. Employees who are not exempt should complete the Personal Allowances Worksheet. Additional worksheets are provided on page 2 for employees to adjust their withholding allowances based on itemized deductions, adjustments to income, or two-earner/two-job situations. Complete all worksheets that apply to your situation. The worksheets will help you figure the number of withholding allowances you are entitled to claim. However, you may claim fewer allowances than this.

Head of Household. Generally, you may claim head of household filing status on your tax return only if you are unmarried and pay more than 50% of the costs of keeping up a home for yourself and your dependent(s) or other qualifying individuals.

Nonwage Income. If you have a large amount of nonwage income, such as interest or dividends, you should consider making estimated tax payments using Form 1040-ES. Otherwise, you may find that you owe additional tax at the end of the year.

Two Earners/Two Jobs. If you have a working spouse or more than one job, figure the total number of allowances you are entitled to claim on all jobs using worksheets from only one Form W-4. This total should be divided among all jobs. Your withholding will usually be most accurate when all allowances are claimed on the W-4 filed for the highest paying job and zero allowances are claimed for the others.

Check Your Withholding. After your W-4 takes effect, you can use **Pub. 919,** Is My Withholding Correct for 1995?, to see how the dollar amount you are having withheld compares to your estimated total annual tax. We recommend you get Pub. 919 especially if you used the Two Earner/Two Job Worksheet and your earnings exceed $150,000 (Single) or $200,000 (Married). Call 1-800-829-3676 to order Pub. 919. Check your telephone directory for the IRS assistance number for further help.

Personal Allowances Worksheet

A Enter "1" for **yourself** if no one else can claim you as a dependent . . . . A ______

B Enter "1" if:
- You are single and have only one job; or
- You are married, have only one job, and your spouse does not work; or
- Your wages from a second job or your spouse's wages (or the total of both) are $1,000 or less.

. . . B ______

C Enter "1" for your **spouse.** But, you may choose to enter -0- if you are married and have either a working spouse or more than one job (this may help you avoid having too little tax withheld) . . . . C ______

D Enter number of **dependents** (other than your spouse or yourself) you will claim on your tax return . . . . D ______

E Enter "1" if you will file as **head of household** on your tax return (see conditions under **Head of Household** above) . E ______

F Enter "1" if you have at least $1,500 of **child or dependent care expenses** for which you plan to claim a credit . . F ______

G Add lines A through F and enter total here. **Note:** This amount may be different from the number of exemptions you claim on your return ▶ G ______

For accuracy, do all worksheets that apply.
- If you plan to **itemize or claim adjustments to income** and want to reduce your withholding, see the Deductions and Adjustments Worksheet on page 2.
- If you are **single** and have **more than one job** and your combined earnings from all jobs exceed $30,000 OR if you are **married** and have a **working spouse or more than one job,** and the combined earnings from all jobs exceed $50,000, see the Two-Earner/Two-Job Worksheet on page 2 if you want to avoid having too little tax withheld.
- If **neither** of the above situations applies, **stop here** and enter the number from line G on line 5 of Form W-4 below.

Cut here and give the certificate to your employer. Keep the top portion for your records.

Form **W-4** Department of the Treasury Internal Revenue Service

Employee's Withholding Allowance Certificate

▶ For Privacy Act and Paperwork Reduction Act Notice, see reverse.

OMB No. 1545-0010 **1995**

1 Type or print your first name and middle initial | Last name | 2 Your social security number

Home address (number and street or rural route) | 3 ☐ Single ☐ Married ☐ Married, but withhold at higher Single rate.
Note: *If married, but legally separated, or spouse is a nonresident alien, check the Single box.*

City or town, state, and ZIP code | 4 If your last name differs from that on your social security card, check here and call 1-800-772-1213 for a new card . . . . . ▶ ☐

5 Total number of allowances you are claiming (from line G above or from the worksheets on page 2 if they apply) . | 5

6 Additional amount, if any, you want withheld from each paycheck . . . . | 6 $

7 I claim exemption from withholding for 1995 and I certify that I meet **BOTH** of the following conditions for exemption:
- Last year I had a right to a refund of **ALL** Federal income tax withheld because I had **NO** tax liability; **AND**
- This year I expect a refund of **ALL** Federal income tax withheld because I expect to have **NO** tax liability.

If you meet both conditions, enter "EXEMPT" here . . . . ▶ | 7

Under penalties of perjury, I certify that I am entitled to the number of withholding allowances claimed on this certificate or entitled to claim exempt status.

Employee's signature ▶ **Date ▶** , 19

8 Employer's name and address (Employer: Complete 8 and 10 only if sending to the IRS) | 9 Office code (optional) | 10 Employer identification number

Cat. No. 10220Q

Fig. 2–13 W-4.

Third, the codification of our program creates a mission statement with teeth. In order to write directions, we must first define the destination. The hows and whys become the wheres and whens, and your office documents become your mission manual.

Fourth, you never want your "brains" to walk out the front door. No matter how long a trusted employee has been with you, there will come a day when she leaves. If running the office depends upon Lucy's business skills, you practice in grave peril. Even before you reach the end of this book, go to the office and ask Lucy to begin writing it down.

STAFF REWARDS

What compensation does it take to hold good staff? I have lost a good employee over my unwillingness to pay another 25 cents an hour. That was pure stupidity. I had not yet learned a major management lesson: It is smarter to retain than retrain.

How much to pay? What benefits to offer? Consider your competition. They know the answers to these questions, for they will draw away the cream of your staff if you don't know what your market takes to attract and hold good team players.

In the 1960s, dentists believed staff should feel privileged just to work in our offices. This privilege was the only benefit offered, and the pay was paltry, even by those standards. Today we know a new truth: The quality of the dental services we offer will never exceed the quality of our staff.

Over the years we have experimented, I suppose, with dozens of different compensation plans. One thing seems sure. We will change as times change. Our chairside assistants now work four weekdays, giving a full weekday off, with one Saturday morning, once a month, and two evenings until 8 P.M. each week.

Those hours only mean something when they equate with what our staff wants and what hours they are willing to work to accomplish their goals.

When we moved into our new office a couple of years ago, I offered to take staff members on a nice vacation if they could meet a production goal that was $250,000 over the best previous year. They could win the trip with any 12 consecutive months of production, meaning each month they counted to see if they had won. It took them

13 months in the new office before 31 of them won a four-day trip to Cancun (Fig. 2–6).

For tax purposes, the trip had an assigned value, and staff members were required to report its value on their income tax returns. We had learned this the hard way. Years ago, when we took a dozen staffers to

IA W4 44-019	Iowa Department of Revenue and Finance IOWA EMPLOYEE'S WITHHOLDING ALLOWANCE CERTIFICATE	625-1037 (Rev. 1/91R)

Print your full name

Social Security Number

Home Address (number and street or rural route)

Marital Status
☐ Single ☐ Married
If married but legally separated, check single.

City, State, Zip

1. Personal allowances ....
2. Allowances for dependents ....
3. Allowances for itemized deductions ....
4. Allowance for child or dependent care credit ....
5. Total allowances (add lines 1 through 4) ....
6. Additional amount, if any, you want deducted each pay period .... $
7. I claim exemption from withholding because (check boxes that apply):

   a. ☐ Last year I did not owe any Iowa income tax and had a right to a full refund of ALL income tax withheld, and

   b. ☐ This year I do not expect to owe any Iowa income tax and expect to have a right to a full refund of ALL income tax withheld. If both "a." and "b." apply, enter the year effective and "EXEMPT" here | Year |

   c. If you entered "EXEMPT" on line 7b, are you a full-time student?   ___ Yes   ___ No

I certify that I am entitled to the number of withholding allowances claimed on this certificate, or if claiming an exemption from withholding, that I am entitled to claim the exempt status.

Employee's Signature   Date

8. Employer's name and address (Employer: Complete 8 and 9 only if sending to Iowa Department of Revenue and Finance.)   9. Employer identification number

DETACH

FILING REQUIREMENTS AND NUMBER OF ALLOWANCES — Each employee must file this certificate with his or her employer. Do not claim more than the correct number of allowances. However, if you expect to owe more income tax for the year than will be withheld, you may increase the withholding by claiming a small number of allowances, or you may enter into an agreement with your employer to have additional amounts withheld.

1. **PERSONAL ALLOWANCES** — You can claim the following personal allowances:

   One allowance for yourself or 2 allowances if you are unmarried and eligible to claim head of household status, 1 allowance if you are 65 or older, and 1 allowance if you are blind.

   If you are married and your spouse either does not work or is not claiming his or her allowances on a separate W-4, you may also claim the following allowances: 1 for your spouse, 1 if your spouse is 65 or older, and 1 if your spouse is blind.

   If you are single and hold more than one job, you may not claim the same allowances with more than one employer at the same time. If you are married and both you and your spouse are employed, you may not both claim the same allowances with both of your employers at the same time. To have the highest amount of tax withheld claim "0" allowances on line 1.

2. **ALLOWANCES FOR DEPENDENTS** — You may claim one allowance for each dependent you will be able to claim on your Iowa income tax return.

3. **ALLOWANCES FOR ITEMIZED DEDUCTIONS** — See reverse side.

4. **ALLOWANCES FOR CHILD/DEPENDENT CARE CREDIT** — See reverse side.

5. **TOTAL** — Enter total of lines 1 through 4

6. **ADDITIONAL AMOUNT OF WITHHOLDING DEDUCTED** — If you are not having enough tax withheld from your pay, you may request your employer to withhold more by filling in an additional amount on line 6. Often married couples, both of whom are working, and persons with two or more jobs need to have additional tax withheld. You may also need to have additional tax withheld because you have income other than wages, such as interest and dividends, capital gains, rents, alimony received, etc. Estimate the amount you will be under withheld, and divide that amount by the number of pay periods in the year.

7. **EXEMPTION FROM WITHHOLDING** — You can claim exemption from withholding only if last year you did not owe any Iowa income tax and had a right to a full refund of all income tax withheld, and this year you do not expect to owe any Iowa income tax and expect to have a right to a refund of all income tax withheld. If you qualify, check boxes "a" and "b", write the year exempt status is effective, and "EXEMPT" on line b, and answer the question on line c.

REVOCATION AND EXPIRATION — You must revoke the exemption from withholding (1) within 10 days from the day you anticipate you will incur an Iowa income tax liability for the calendar year (or your fiscal tax year) or (2) on or before December 31, if you anticipate you will incur an Iowa income tax liability for the following year.

If you want to discontinue or are required to revoke this certificate, you must file a new Iowa Employee's Withholding Allowance Certificate with your employer.

If you want to claim an exemption from withholding next year, you must file a new W-4 with your employer on or before February 15.

CHANGES IN ALLOWANCES — You may file a new certificate at any time if the number of your allowances INCREASES. You must file a new certificate within 10 days if the number of allowances previously claimed by you DECREASES.

PENALTIES — Penalties are imposed for willfully supplying false information or willful failure to supply information which would reduce the withholding allowances. If you file as exempt from withholding and you incur an income tax liability, you may be subject to a penalty for underpayment of estimated tax.

EMPLOYER REQUIREMENTS — The employer must maintain records of the certificates. If the employee is claiming more than 22 withholding allowances or claiming exemption from withholding when wages are expected to exceed $200 a week, the employer must send a copy of the certificate under separate cover within ninety days to the Individual Section, Audit and Compliance Division, Iowa Department of Revenue and Finance, P.O. Box 10456, Hoover State Office Building, Des Moines, Iowa 50306.

121

Fig. 2–14 State employee's withholding allowance certificate.

Hawaii to the ADA meeting, the IRS ruled the trip was a vacation and therefore a staff bonus. My IRS audit cost me roughly $75,000. We will not allow that to recur.

There are many ways to give staff bonuses. Some offices award bonuses to different staff members on various formulas. That seems strange, particularly in light of the current fad for team playing. It seems to me that if the office is to truly experience teamwork, goals should reflect the efforts of the entire team, not fractions thereof.

In a similar vein, I fail to understand how doctors can put the burden of profits on staff. Isn't a profitable operation the responsibility of management? It seems to me that a team-playing staff will find ways to save money. A staff member who is given $20 now for a smart office idea, can be more motivated by cash than by a year-end promise.

I can almost understand bonuses for collections, although it's the doctor's responsibility to establish programs that bring in the money. Bonuses for production are good enough for me. Get the production, and I'll figure out how to get collections and make profits.

Office bonuses are tricky things. The danger comes from starting programs in slow times that you cannot live with in good times. For example, some doctors will sell their soul for (pick one or more) more new patients, more gross production, more net production, greater veneer sales, more denture sales, or more cosmetic procedures.

The problem comes when the program works. They get more of whatever and find the bonus program they instituted becomes a chain around their necks, and they are forever trapped, having given away much too much in receipt for much too little.

A dentist came up to me after an all-day lecture and asked if we could go off alone somewhere and talk. We found a quiet place and he unloaded. His practice was incredibly good, had grown by leaps and bounds, enjoyed a wonderful new patient flow, and he claimed that his team was the world's best.

There was only one flaw in his plan. Back in the days when he hungered for success, he made a deal with the devil. He offered pricey bonuses for new business. It worked. He got the business, more than he had dreamed possible, but he did not know how to stop the bonuses that became crippling. He was trapped, and he faced bankruptcy because of a successful practice, an incredible dichotomy, but real.

Several years ago, I gave out Christmas bonuses at year-end. The cash-flow drain became critical and I wanted to spread the bonus out over the year, rather than have it dump into my finances on one day. The alternative we offered was not only acceptable, but met with smiles.

"Debbie, I've got a deal for you," I told a senior staffer. "I'm going to give you a raise in exchange for your Christmas bonus. That way, you will earn extra every payday, rather than having me save it for you for Christmas."

Debbie had received an $800 bonus the year before. She had worked roughly 1,800 hours, meaning her bonus per hour was about 44 cents. The raise we offered was 50 cents per hour and she was delighted. She would get the cash all year. I told her it was her raise for the year, which meant my labor costs were fixed. Spreading the bonus over the year removed the year-end cash-flow drain. We all smiled.

Here are some bonus quick tips: Start no bonus you can't live with in really good times. Reward the team, not the players. Set a deadline. Make it attainable. Don't put the payday too far in the future. Use your imagination. Have fun. Remember the key attitude about bonuses: Dentists who try to keep all the profits never earn up to their potential.

EDUCATION, TO BE CONTINUED

Here's a drill for you, doctor. Call your office and ask, "How much do you charge for a filling?" If you have two people or more who answer the phone, call again and ask the same question.

The answers you receive may not reflect your office philosophy. They may not be consistent. The question then is how to achieve consistently correct telephone answers. Train our staff, right? How?

There's something wrong with a system of continuing education that works like the current haphazard system. For years, we have trained a staff member when she arrives on the job. We hold regular staff meetings, require staff to read the training manual each year, and then we hope a lot.

The current method of raising the quality of dental office performance is haphazard, at best, and aimless or chaotic, at worst. If dentists were taught in dental school the way we teach our staff, think where the profession would be today.

Analyze why these training methods fall short. Initial training, when a new staff member arrives on the scene, is usually hurried and flurried. Too many subjects must be covered. The fine points, the nuances, the finesse that dental jobs require can never be taught in two-week training periods. How then?

The training manual kicks in. A training manual is critical, but relying on it for ongoing training is chancy. People often don't care to read, their minds go blank or they have many demands on them and concentration is difficult. There are no quizzes, no checks and balances.

Staff meetings are not much better. These sessions often turn out to be force feeding, rather than educational feasting. Our last hope is that staff members will receive adequate on-the-job training from other staffers. A few staffers may even receive feedback from displeased patients, a terrible way to learn an important lesson.

Don't misunderstand. My criticism of staff training methods is not directed at your office. I am criticizing our GD office methods as much as the profession's approach to continuing education of the people we want to represent us.

Wouldn't we like our team to maybe sell some dentistry, make some useful financial plans, and give our patients a feel-good dental experience? As a minimum, wouldn't it be nice if they just don't misrepresent us? Some days that's a high enough goal.

Most of us admire the team that surrounds our days, fills our dental chairs, and paves the path to prosperity. Don't they deserve better tools than the ones we've given them? I think so.

Introductory training must be done, of course, but where are the follow-up training videos? There are no shortages of topics: patient care, telephone response, answering questions, financial arranging, treatment plan presentation, informed consents, and even material handling. In the marketplace, wondrous technology does a better job creating aimless games for idle teens than it does useful training for dental teams. That's one weakness.

Attitude adjustment during staff meetings may have important value. Sooner or later, however, the steam we generate has to move a flywheel and result in useful work. When overdone, steam generation can be just more hot air.

Another kind of staff meeting is the kind I've observed in my office for years. Staff assembles, an agenda is presented, the meeting coordinator walks through the agenda, and a group discussion is held on those management-selected topics. There is a certain sham about these meetings that pretend staff is participating in the decision-making process. I doubt if anyone is fooled by that pretense.

Meetings of this sort are pyramidal. That is, I see them as the boss sitting atop the pyramid, shouting orders down to those below. It's the classroom we all were schooled in, but I doubt if it is the best teaching/learning method.

What if we asked staff members to teach themselves? How would that work? Here's where I got the idea.

In 1922, Carl Seashore, a University of Iowa professor (who invented the discipline of speech pathology), announced that a creative essay would be acceptable for a graduate degree. From that inception, the Iowa Writers' Workshop sprang, based on the premise that writers could be encouraged, if not produced.

The workshops's philosophy was simple. Bring a group of wannabe writers together and have the group—under the guidance of a published writer—critique the members' works. The concept worked so well it has become the pattern for writers' workshops the world over.

Since the concept is proven, why wouldn't this work in dentistry, as well? I would like to tell you we have used this successfully for years, and it works. I would like to tell you that, but if I did it wouldn't be true. We are just embarking on a new training method, based on the workshop idea. Here's how we work it.

We select a topic to be studied, perhaps it is standardizing our telephone responses to routine questions callers ask. The group of trainees gathers, and a tape recording of an unidentified caller asking a question is played. The group listens and then critiques the respondent, whose voice is recognizable to all.

Maybe the topic is for chairside assistants and we want to study how to develop consistently correct and useful printed treatment plans. A tape is played of a doctor calling out his exam findings and diagnosis. A chairside assistant charts the findings as he calls them out, then goes to a terminal and creates a treatment plan, which is printed and critiqued by other chairside assistants.

Notice the difference. When staff teaches staff, rather than receiving dictums from on high, the team concept could hardly be better served. Now, everyone is inspired to help all of the team reach a higher quality of care.

In our discussion of staff—attracting, screening, hiring, firing, self-protection, documentation, bonuses, retaining, and training—we have yet to reflect on averages. The reason is simple. There is nothing average about excellence, and achieving it requires the pain-for-gain trade-off.

Developing techniques to teach staff is one thing but having staff teach me is quite another. Sometimes their methods, while seemingly abrupt, carry a message one never forgets. I've had several such experiences that are seared into my mind. When you've read them, you may see that they carry lessons worth knowing.

LESSON ONE

My receptionist buzzed me on the intercom and told me that a man was at the front desk asking to see me. The genial gentleman smiled, introduced himself as Sam, and showed me the badge of an inspector for the Iowa Board of Pharmacy Examiners. We sat down in my private office, and he said they had been alerted by a national drug warehouse about what seemed to be excessive drug purchases.

"Dr. Schmidt, can you account for the purchase of over 20,000 Tylenol 3's during the past three years?"

"You say 20,000?" My stomach did flipflops. I conducted Sam on a tour of our facility, and he inspected how we stored and locked our drugs. He noted our security measures met all federal and state security laws.

At that time, clinical notes were a dream for the future, so in order to find an answer we physically inspected and counted roughly thousands of charts. The job took three days. When Sam returned, I gave him the news he expected.

"We can only account for a few thousand."

Reporting this incident as fairly as I can, despite my prejudice, the upshot was that my rover, who placed all orders, had continued to order

1,000-pill containers of Tylenol 3, even when monthly disappearances of drugs far exceeded drugs dispensed. It was an oversight on her part for not picking up on the thefts, which they must have been. It was pure neglect on my part to not know of the losses.

The theft was probably committed by someone who had access to drugs inside the office—staff, staff friend, or cleaning crew. We never knew who. Three of us passed lie detector tests. Some staff and doctors refused to be tested, which was their right, and for some reason they soon left our employ.

A reward for information leading to the discovery of the thief produced a late-night phone call from a person who asked $10,000 to give me the name of the thief. Had I produced the thief, I might have been held guiltless, given the inspector's notation of adequate security.

In retrospect, $10,000 may have been a worthwhile investment. On the other hand, it might have only played into a con game.

The Iowa Board of Dental Examiners found me guilty of failing to have appropriate professional control and they suspended my license for one month. The attendant publicity was, as expected, humiliating (Figs. 2–15, 2–16).

Lessons learned? Don't keep inventory of any controlled substances. There are people who will do anything to get them, including destroying you in the process. Keep on top of all purchases. Develop a preventive system of checks and balances. Ten thousand dollars might have been an inexpensive out.

LESSON TWO

The letter was marked "Certified Mail, return receipt requested." It was handed to me as I conducted a hygiene exam. The return address bore the imprint of the Iowa Board of Dental Examiners. Even recalling that curdling moment puts terror in my gut.

What happened next was the deepest wound of my career. The circumstance might have happened to anyone. Lessons learned are as serious in a small office as in a large one.

The document from the board charged me with a multitude of sins in the form of illegal practices. Several avowed witnesses were listed by

Dentist plans license appeal; offers reward for capture of drug thieves

Dr. Duane Schmidt has filed a court document indicating he plans to appeal the 30-day suspension of his license to practice as a dentist in Iowa.

The document, an application for a stay order, was filed in Linn Board of dental Court Thursday. It seeks an order stopping the suspension until after he has a chance to challenge it in court.

The suspension, effective next Monday, was imposed by the Iowa Board of Dental Examiners after Schmidt's office, in Cedar Rapids, was audited by the Iowa Board of Parmacy Exaiminers.

That investigation revealed five "diversions" of drugs containing codeine from the office between Jan. 16, 1984, and Jan. 30, 1985. The investigator reported them to the Cedar Rapids Police Department as an employee theft.

Among the dental board's accusations was that Schmidt didn't report the theft's to the board and failed to take effective to stop them.

A news release from Schmidt includes the following statements:

"Since security on these drugs complied with all federal and state laws, and since there was no sign of break-in, it is unknown how the thefts occurred. Several employees, including Dr. Schmidt, have passed polygraph tests and cooperated with agents in attempts to bring the culprit to justice.

"For a victim of a crime to be held responsible for a crime having been committed escapes all logic. Dental East will offer a $1,000 reward for information leading to arrest and conviction of the person or persons responsible for the thefts."

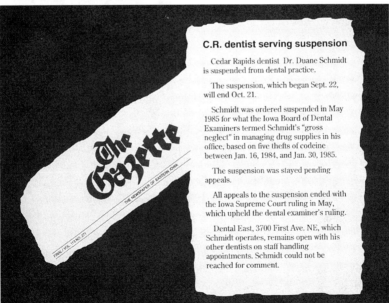

C.R. dentist serving suspension

Cedar Rapids dentist Dr. Duane Schmidt is suspended from dental practice.

The suspension, which began Sept. 22, will end Oct. 21.

Schmidt was ordered suspended in May 1985 for what the Iowa Board of Dental Examiners termed Schmidt's "gross neglect" in managing drug supplies in his office, based on five thefts of codeine between Jan. 16, 1984, and Jan. 30, 1985.

The suspension was stayed pending appeals.

All appeals to the suspension ended with the Iowa Supreme Court ruling in May, which upheld the dental examiner's ruling.

Dental East, 3700 First Ave. NE, which Schmidt operates, remains open with his other dentists on staff handling appointments. Schmidt could not be reached for comment.

Figs. 2–15, 2–16 News clippings of Dr. Duane A. Schmidt's license suspension announcement.

initials, which we deciphered to be former dental assistants in our office. The charges ranged from having an unsterile office to allowing a hygienist to perform anesthetic injections, and from allowing assistants to place fillings to writing prescriptions for nondental reasons.

Professional liability insurance does not provide defense against these charges. After six agonizing months, and more than $12,000 later, my attorneys negotiated a settlement with the board for a two-month suspension of my license in exchange for dropping the charges. (Fig. 2–17)

Was that a smart move? My attorneys convinced me it was because of my former conflict with the board in the Tylenol 3 thefts. They believed that despite our ability to absolutely disprove many of these current charges, the board might not be willing to settle for a two-month suspension, after holding a full-blown hearing. Counsel estimated that costs for the hearing, plus depositions and witness testimony, would run another $20,000.

Was I guilty? Good question. No, a hygienist did not inject an anesthetic. A first-day, dental assistant student saw a hygienist apply sealant, with what might look like a syringe to a novice. The student incorrectly assumed the hygienist injected an anesthetic, when nothing could have been further from the truth.

Prescriptions for "nondental" drugs were for TMJ muscle relaxants written in consultation with my patient's physician. We had a letter on file from the physician to that effect. The investigator, however, took the word of an untrained assistant as gospel. She made a formal charge, without asking what, when, or why of me.

Not only was our "unsterile" office OSHA-compliant, but we had been cited in an article in the *Journal of the American Dental Association* (JADA, January 1992) for being the first dental office in the nation to pass an OSHA inspection without a single violation of a bloodborne pathogen standard. At the time, we were told that no dental college had passed an OSHA exam.

As to charges of allowing assistants to perform illegal activities, that one was going to be tougher to fight. Our defense difficulty stemmed from the purported witnesses, apparently willing to vote in block about such things as holding impressions, removing flash around temporary crowns, and the like.

I accepted the settlement, and went to Europe for a two-month driving trip, from Munich to the Arctic Circle, above Sweden and Finland, down to the rock of Gibraltar, and back to Paris. I had a great deal of anger to drive away on the 7,000-mile trip. Some of it left. It was the supreme test of my Sooper days. The test succeeded.

A few days after I returned to my practice, Charlene, a chairside assistant of several years, came into my private office, closed the door, and broke down in tears. I asked her what was wrong, and she said, "Dr. Schmidt, I've done something so terrible I cannot live with it any longer. My husband said I should have the courage to tell you."

I was appropriately flummoxed and said so.

"I was one of the assistants who witnessed against you to the board. I went along with it because my friend asked me to help her hurt you. We made up the charges. I know you are going to fire me, but I have to get this off my mind."

I was dumbfounded. Of course, I knew the charges were trumped up. I had pieced together their genesis. The previous year, Winifred, another chairside assistant, had become pregnant and decided she would not take X-rays. We told her she was protected by the X-ray room walls, the button was outside the room, and our X-ray machines are annually tested and collimated by the Iowa Department of Public Health. Zero stray radiation was our proven standard.

We pointed out that all staff members who take X-rays are required to quarterly wear the test badge, develop the film themselves, and save it on file. No assistant had ever failed any of the tests, and dozens of employees had gone through successful pregnancies, taking patient X-rays until the day they delivered.

Winifred would not accept that, and she quit, filing for unemployment compensation. Our protest of unemployment pay was upheld, and one now-vengeful former employee planned revenge. Winifred enlisted several other past employees, along with Charlene, to abet her cause. Working on half-truths and leading questions, they developed the scenario of charges.

"What will you do?" Charlene asked, between sobs.

I offered her a tissue and said, "Well, I won't fire someone honest enough to tell me the truth. Charlene, I thought I knew what happened, but without your honesty, I would have always wondered. Your job is safe."

"But what should I do?" she asked.

"Whatever you feel is right. If you want to tell the board, it would be nice."

She wrote the letter and my attorney presented it to the board. The answer? The board does not review past decisions. Period.

The lesson learned? The same I learned as a Boy Scout. Be prepared.

Now, each quarter, staff must sign notarized statements asserting they have not been involved in any illegal activities, have not seen anything illegal going on in the office, and know of no illegalities. With these documents under lock and key, we accumulate a continuous body of proof with which to quash future disasters.

Can you learn from my mistakes? Good question. Sometimes, I've failed to learn from my own mistakes, so it's a toss-up. If I can impress you with how desperate situations can arise from seemingly innocent events, perhaps yes. One can be right, as we were in winning denial of unemployment pay, and lose heavily, if we have exposed an unprotected flank.

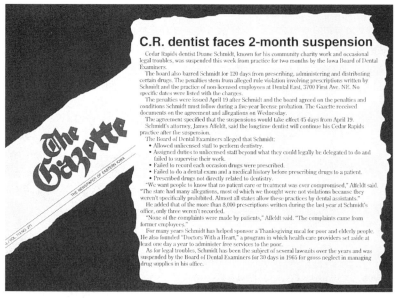

Fig. 2–17 News clipping of Dr. Duane A. Schmidt's two-month license suspension.

Did I lose respect for my team because of this incident? Not for a moment. These friends and I have worked together for years, many for as much as a decade and a half. We all know there are bad people who will do bad things. Sometimes laws seem to support evil. In the final analysis, I am convinced that—in the Iowa idiom—all chickens come home to roost.

The staff/team is so important to practice success that time spent dealing with these issues is never enough, but we have to move on. There are other valuable things planned for *Schmidt's Anatomy* and I don't want to short them. I want to report our OSHA episode and how you can profit from that experience. Our electronic dental office (EDO) reveals fresh approaches to dentistry. In addition, I want to go into my decades of experience in successful marketing and selling, financial and treatment planning, and management measures to show how we keep score.

Today, various state dental practice acts that deal with allowable duties for dental assistants range from holding them to be mere spit-suckers to allowing expanded function assistants (EFA) to actually use their brains. While physicians have nurses and medical assistants, dentistry dallies in the past.

The ADA must exercise leadership to promote national standards for the profession of dental assisting. The twentieth century is nearly history everywhere except in many state dental practice acts. It's time we got with it, ladies and gentlemen. The dismal pattern of governmental interference has always been clear: Where we fear to tread, the public will walk in.

DISSECTION LAB

In Chapter Two we have discussed key players in the dental office and how to get and hold them. Smart dentists sensibly employ people who work well together, have purpose, direction, and accept the dentist's role of leader.

In our emphasis on staff we can forget that a strong staff will not correct weak leadership. The pivotal figure in every equation is the equal sign. The dentist is the equalizer in every dental office equation.

In this chapter we examined:

- Attracting staff applicants.

- Interviewing from the first call.

- The application process.

- The value of screening out.

  - Do not hire overqualified applicants.

  - Do not hire applicants with spouse job instability.

  - Do not hire applicants who do not speak well of former employers.

- "Three people to please" speech to new staff.

- Winning attributes: Personality and comeliness.

- Bringing new staff on line.

- Conditional employment agreements.

- An in-office notary public.

- Biohazardous waste acknowledgment agreement.

- New Team Member's Statement of Knowledge.

- Giving up the right to sue.

- Quarterly Team Member's Statement of Knowledge.

- Various other important sign-on documents.

- Similarities all dental offices share.

- Assembling start-up documentation menus.

- Staff rewards.

- Office education, to be continued.

Dentists who try to keep all the profits will never make as much as they should.

THE WORLD'S FIRST WOMAN DENTIST

In the mid-1800s, dentists apprenticed just like a blacksmith or barber. They looked over the shoulder of another dentist until they learned how to perform extractions and restorations.

Lucy Hobbs learned to be a dentist that way. She was so good at it that her fellow dentists in McGregor, Iowa, urged her to attend one of the five dental colleges in the United States. She chose Ohio College in Cincinnati.

In 1865, Lucy Hobbs graduated with the degree of Doctor of Dental Surgery, not only one of the first 65 graduate dentists, but the first woman in history to hold that degree. Following graduation, she returned to Iowa where she practiced for several years.

CHAPTER THREE

---◆---

THE
BLOOD-VASCULAR
SYSTEM

Jerry seemed like a such a well-mannered, pleasant young man, but we knew he held frightening power in his briefcase. When I was told he had arrived at the GD front desk, I personally escorted him into my private office and called my daughter Catherine to join us. We had expected his visit, yet we fervently hoped he would never arrive.

The *Journal of the American Dental Association* had told us he would be there one day. Our gut instincts told us he would find us among the first. After all, we were the largest, the best example he could find.

One is never prepared well enough for death, divorce, or deadly disease. Similarly, no dental office is ever prepared well enough for a visit from . . . OSHA. Jerry represented the Iowa Division of Labor Services. Catherine Schmidt, R.D.H., awaiting the results of her CRDT exams—so that she could begin practice in our office—had accepted the role of GD Exposure Control Manager. The conversation went something like this:

"I'm here to conduct an OSHA examination of your office, Dr. Schmidt."

"Why?" I asked, buying time.

"You have been charged with five alleged safety or health hazards," he said, smiling broadly at us. "Would you like me to produce a search warrant?" Jerry looked and acted innocuous and gracious, but Cathy and I knew full well—given the viral and bacterial hysteria of those turbulent days—he held the power to close GD as easily as he shut his briefcase.

The AIDS-frenzied 1990s were not halcyon times. With Jerry's sanction, our name could become today's dirt in the local media. Moreover, reports in the dental press had clearly warned that an OSHA inspection could mean bankruptcy. To that time, no dentist had escaped the hammer of fines, horrible press, and surely practice slowdown following a negative report from an OSHA inspection. No dental college had endured an OSHA examination without being trashed, sometimes with fines in the tens of thousands of dollars.

"Yes, yes, we'll waive the search warrant." No point in antagonizing him over something that would only be an irritant, not a deterrent. "May we see the charges?" we asked.

"Of course." He handed us a list of five items. They apparently were typed in the words of the claimant. The list read (exact spelling and punctuation preserved):

HEALTH:

1. The labs pumus pan is used all day long and does not get cleaned at the end of the day. It hasn't been cleaned in the last month.

2. Hand pieces are only autoclaved if they have blood on them.

3. Doctor only wears gloves when doing surgery. Other employees wear face shields but are not allowed to wear face masks or lab coats because the doctor does not want the patients to feel as if they are in a dental office. He also feels that protective equipment is not necessary.

4. Coffee pot and cups for staffers is located in sterile lab.

SAFETY:

1. Lab downstairs (dentures, crowns etc) has only one exit. The windows would be very hard to get out.

"Who made these charges?" I asked, nodding to the list.

Jerry shook his head. "Sorry, can't reveal the source." How convenient, I thought.

I mentally pondered our recent $25,000 investment in sterilizers, new handpieces, gowns, training, and barrier equipment and wondered where these rules would cease.

Those thoughts were academic but this was a real circumstance. I could almost hear Catherine's brain clicking at lightning speed. She had been on a three-month, full-time pursuit of OSHA compliance, acquiring training tools, buying new equipment, and gowning the entire staff. She had changed our method of operation and spent dozens of hours training all of us.

Our office—just like all of dentistry—had been gearing up for OSHA compliance since earlier in the year, when the July 7 deadline had been announced. We accepted the fact that compliance was the law of the land. We expected to be among the first to be tested because, as a mega-dental office, we were always tested first on any major change in rulings. It all came down to this exact, terrifying moment.

Cathy's first question, when I asked her to become our first Exposure Control Manager, was, "What's my budget?"

"Anything you need," was my instant answer. How smart would it be to risk huge fines, public humiliation, and loss of market position—possibly jeopardizing the future of GD—by coming up short on our OSHA compliance program? Never a consideration.

The cost of OSHA compliance was our guarantee of being in business tomorrow. It's called survival, not cost.

"How do you intend to conduct your examination, Jerry?" Cathy asked.

He said he would first examine all the written documents, then he would go through the office, from top to bottom. We had three stories with business offices and staff lounge on the top floor, treatment areas on the main floor, and denture and ceramic labs in the basement. We knew the inspector was required to inspect only the scope of the complaint, but he would certainly not walk through the office with eyes closed.

Jerry said he would then watch dental procedures in the operatories and hold private interviews with staff members. Cath and I must have reached the same conclusion at once. We both saw an opening.

"Jerry, we don't let visitors in our operatory. That would invade our patients' privacy. That's out of the question," Cathy said.

I added, "And I will have to be present when you conduct your interviews." I was really scared, although I hid it well. Turning this meeting into a confrontational dispute was a gamble that could be a huge mistake.

The decision about how much to resist any governmental body, from the IRS to a state board, hinges on your perception of your rights and your willingness to stand up for them. Standing up for perceived rights against some public officials could be a fatal mistake. These decisions are never easy calls.

"Dr. Schmidt, that's not possible. I must observe your procedures and how they are conducted. And you definitely cannot be in on staff interviews," Jerry continued, his smile intact.

"Then I guess we have a problem here, Jerry." I looked him squarely in the eye. "How do you propose we resolve it?" Cathy and I didn't know the answer. Maybe he did.

Jerry asked to use a phone and, as he spoke privately with his office, Cathy and I quickly discussed our strategy. Our plan was simple: Involve the ADA as much as they would accept, and keep doing exactly as we had been, to prepare the office and the staff for this cataclysmic event.

In a few minutes, he returned and suggested that the state attorney for OSHA should call and inform us of the law. We told him that, since we had an attorney (we assumed it would be through the ADA), our disagreement should be solved at the attorney level.

"Fine. I'll have my attorney call your attorney and let's let them work out the details. Okay?" We may have been the first dental office he had inspected. He might have been feeling his way, too.

Jerry seemed as relieved as we now felt, knowing we had forestalled the inspection. We traded names and telephone numbers of our attorneys, about like people do at the scene of an accident. Jerry shook hands, smiled again and left. He certainly seemed like a nice, congenial guy.

When he left, Cathy and I just looked at each other and exhaled. We didn't speak. Finally, from a sheaf of papers, she pulled out a recent staff notice she had written.

"Here, read this, Dad." The notice, which she had posted for staff only three weeks earlier, read:

> Staff, you may be assured that GD will be among the first dental offices in the nation to have an OSHA inspection. Here's how we are going to prepare for it . . ."

I laughed, "Nice call, Cathy." Then we got busy. The first order of business was to address the severity of the charges, discover what, if any, substance there was to them, and try to figure out who made them.

Prior to July 7, none of the charges had been illegal. Yet, the document was dated July 7. The question became: How could an employee, on the exact date of July 7, see the supposed violations, then file a charge in Des Moines, two-and-a-half hours' drive from Cedar Rapids? It was virtually an impossible scenario.

The date seemed to indicate these charges were assembled earlier, then saved to be made on that exact date. Most dental assistants, particularly those unable to spell pumice (pumus?), would not have been aware of the special significance of July 7, when new OSHA laws took effect.

The complainant marked a box which indicated she had brought these conditions to the attention of the employer. Impossible. We had not been told. Just another lie, but as the ADA points out, even spiteful charges must be answered.

Cathy and I brought the office administrator into our guessing game. Our office administrator remembered a recent student intern who had worked for us for a few weeks. We had dismissed her for failing to show up for work/study at scheduled times. Her anger and low dental I.Q. made it likely she was the person seeking vengeance.

Why did it matter who turned us in? An OSHA inspection based upon a complaint must be confined to three things:

1. The charges,

2. Items seen on random walk-through, and

3. Discoveries learned during staff interviews.

If the informant was currently on staff, she would naturally be chosen for an interview by the inspector. At that time, if she realized we might escape penalty—because of compliance or because her charges didn't hold water—she might trump up additional charges. We had our hands full answering charges. Being blindsided during the inspection could tip the scales against us, no matter how right we were.

Our first job was to call Ms. Kathleen Todd, J.D., ADA Division of Legal Affairs, assistant general counsel. She was responsible for helping dentists become OSHA-compliant and immediately rose to the occasion. She offered to fax any materials we might need and call Jerry's attorney. Her moral support, as well as her legal backup, during this ugly time, was exactly what we needed.

From May to mid-July, Cathy had devoted hundreds of hours to our OSHA-compliance readiness. That work was about to pay off, particularly with staff, for they felt part of the process, not pawns in the process. Staff attitudes feed down from how dentists adjust their own attitudes, and both the success of the practice and success during an OSHA inspection depend on a healthy balance between staff and doctor attitudes.

The role of exposure control manager, in teaching staff how to deal with bloodborne pathogens, cannot be understated. Further, Cathy defined the role as an ombudsperson for staff. She gave them someone to talk to who could calm their fears and understand their concerns. It is better for the staff to know they have someone to help shoulder their cares than to feel they have to go outside the office for information, succor, or even worse, for reprieve.

During the weeks of preparation, Cathy bombarded the staff with notices focusing on known safety factors, such as telling them that no dental assistant had ever gotten AIDS in the dental environment. While history has shown that the HIV/AIDS viruses are not virulent concerns in the dental office, the disease entity referred to as "afrAIDS" is highly contagious.

There is no vaccine for that disease either. Cathy also taught awareness and defense against other pathogens, such as hepatitis, TB, and venereal disease.

As we continued our preparations, which had now reached fever pitch, we assured ourselves that the charges were woven of whole cloth. At the same time, Cathy developed a dialogue between Ms. Todd and Jerry, hammering out an agreement we eventually could live with.

She agreed to allow the inspector to observe patient care from a distance, appropriately dressed in OSHA-compliant garb. We asked him to appear to be a visiting dentist, rather than an OSHA inspector. He was not to reveal his mission to any of our patients during his visit.

If our patients knew he was in our office to inspect our sterilizing techniques, a wrong signal might be sent to the community. A worst-case scenario had a patient starting the rumor, "Did you hear that OSHA had to check Gentle Dental because they don't sterilize their dental tools?" No office needs that sort of gossip floating around town.

Cathy also obtained agreement from OSHA to have a staff representative present during an interview, if the staff member requested it. I could not be the staff representative, so the staff promptly elected Cathy to that position.

The GD/ADA/OSHA negotiations, and dealing with staff fears and training, required consummate skill. Noting that Cathy conducted both series of events in a skillful manner goes beyond paternal pride. Ms. Todd noted the same thing in her JADA article, which appeared several months after the ordeal.

One morning, Jerry and his boss—both industrial hygienists—showed up unannounced to begin what was to become a six-hour inspection. We provided them with doctors' jackets so they would appear to be visiting dentists, rather than government officials.

The inspection began by studying GD documentation, records Cathy had spent hundreds of hours compiling. A walk-through inspection took place next, with Cathy dogging them every foot of the way. She wanted to be sure they stayed within the limits of the agreed-upon terms. As patient care permitted, I joined the entourage and answered questions.

There was nothing humorous about their visit, but once, when the group was in our dental lab, Jerry popped a mint in his mouth Cathy quietly said to him, "Jerry, we don't allow eating in the lab areas." He turned crimson and smiled that nice smile. Knowledge is always power.

A dozen staff members were interviewed, with six asking to have Cathy be in on the interview and six asking to be interviewed privately. We informed staff that they had rights, which were to refuse an interview, to refuse to answer any question asked, to be accompanied by the staff representative, and to be interviewed privately. Just as we had fought for office rights, it was important to let staff members know they had rights.

The inspectors were as nice as Jerry had been all during the negotiations, and we felt pretty good about how things had gone. They congratulated our preparedness and complimented our office. Still, there were so many unknowns, and we hadn't seen their final report.

Now it was time to wait—days, weeks, months. Finally, in November, Cathy came bursting into my private office. "Dad! Guess what! Jerry just called!" She paused, surely for dramatic effect. I held my breath in and my palms up.

"We didn't have a single violation of a bloodborne pathogen standard!" she screamed.

We shouted and hugged, and hearing the ruckus, staff joined us in cheers. Coupled with relief was an immense sense of pride over Cathy's accomplishment, and I was proud of our GD staff who had met this crisis with solid teamwork.

Cathy reported the results to the ADA and learned we were considered to be the first dental office to completely pass an OSHA inspection. When Cathy suggested our victory came from a large team working together on compliance, Ms. Todd countered, "On the contrary, Cathy. Your large office gave you even greater opportunities to fail."

One of the first things we did after the inspection was write out Cathy's plan for OSHA compliance. That narrative provided Ms. Todd with advice to pass along to our colleagues.

The next year, we left that OSHA-compliant office and moved into our current 8,000-square-foot building. When we were settled in, Cathy called Jerry and asked for a voluntary inspection. Why? When an office requests inspection, no fines are levied so long as violations discovered during the inspection are corrected within 30 days.

If you have an inkling that your office may be charged with violations, or that it is a prime target for inspection, ask for it before it asks for you. The pressure is off and the penalties almost nonexistent.

The lessons we learned? Of course, infection barrier programs are important and enrich staff knowledge. As Cathy has written, "OSHA compliance is not a bad thing if we view the process for its team-building merits." In retrospect, I agree.

Here's my call for action: The ADA's lobbying effort to resist bodacious OSHA compliance rules, to keep the membership informed, and to develop staff training materials, is exemplary. Be a member and support the ADA, if for no other reason, for these reasons alone.

HE INVENTED LIE-DOWN DENTISTRY

The next time you sit next to your patient, working four-handedly, thank Iowan John Naughton. He invented it all.

Few professional revolutions have been spurred by a single person, especially someone outside the profession. Fortunately, John Naughton didn't know that.

John came up the hard, sales way, selling many door-to-door items, until he became the state distributor for a massage unit that fitted onto an armchair. As a beginning dentist, I clearly recall John inviting us to sit in a bank of his chairs at the Iowa Dental Association annual meetings, where we would lose our convention floor cares in his comfortable chairs.

Dr. Bernard "Barney" Morgan, of Britt, Iowa, and Dr. Meigs Jones of Kansas City, cornered him one day and asked him to build a new dental chair, a chair that would be similar to his comfortable armchairs.

John thought it sounded challenging, so he constructed a prototype and took it to Barney's office, spending a day watching the tall Dr. Morgan work on patients lying on this wonderful idea.

Even though Barney was cramped working over this new chair, he knew his patients loved it, so he immediately ordered another. John said he must first go back to the drawing board and make some changes.

He rebuilt the chair and plowed through a blizzard to Kansas City, to watch his new concept at work in Meigs Jones' office. The next day, the *Kansas City Star* carried a feature story about the startling new concept of dental patients lying down.

John returned to Des Moines and formed the Den-Tal-Ez dental chair manufacturing company, and began the scramble for dentist recognition. At first, dental supply houses refused to show and sell this strange chair. But an even greater problem was the resistance he encountered from dentists entrenched in the stand-up concept of dentistry.

To achieve recognition of his chair, John sent teams of salesmen fanning across the nation to teach dentists the new technique of "four-handed" dentistry. The learning session I attended was held in a St. Albans, Iowa, hotel room.

When dentists objected that patients might choke in the new horizontal position, John pointed out that the throat closes when a person is supine. Dentists were amazed to learn this truth from John, a man who had no medical training.

In a few years, John's chairs became the industry standard, and the lie-down dental concept dominated the dental profession.

Today, dentists live healthier and longer lives, and patients have far brighter dental experiences because of John Naughton, who dared to dream differently.

DISSECTION LAB

OSHA compliance training can be an excellent method of establishing teamwork in the office and protecting staff. OSHA means business, and if you mean to stay in business, you can rail about the injustice of protecting staff and forgetting patients all you wish, but comply. If you want to change the law, support the ADA in the fight for sanity in sanitation laws.

Train, train, then train the team some more. Educate staff. Hide nothing. When nitrous-oxide scavenging equipment first came out, I didn't believe it was all that necessary and failed to tell staff about this option, thinking I might save a dollar.

If I had taken the initiative, I might have turned what happened next into a plus, by simply going out and buying the scavenger. Instead, staff members discovered the scavenging concept and believed it might make for safer staff pregnancies. At once they begged for the hookups and we purchased them.

Upon answering a charge of OSHA noncompliance (Fig. 3–1), inspectors are permitted to view documentation, inspect areas in question, interview random staff members, and only casually inspect the remainder of the office.

Staff members may refuse OSHA interviews, refuse to answer questions, and request a staff representative accompany them in the interview.

Rules, laws, and interpretations of laws change constantly. Today, our inspection might not go as it did then. As a member of the ADA, always consult with the ADA legal staff for current advice. Do not act on your own without good counsel.

Notice of Alleged Safety or Health Hazards | **Iowa Division of Labor Services**
Occupational Safety and Health Bureau

MOD Date
| 7/07/92 |

1. Complaint Number ▶ **73189185**

2. Employer Name
Dental East

3. Site Location (Street City State ZIP)
3700 1st Avenue N.E.   Cedar Rapids   IA 52402

4. Mailing Address (If different) (Street City State ZIP)
3700 1st Avenue N.E.   Cedar Rapids   IA 52402

5. Management Official
Dr. Duane Schmidt

6. Telephone Number
319-366-0767

7. Type of Business
Dental Office

8. Hazard Description Describe briefly the hazard(s) which you believe exist Include the approximate number of employees exposed to or threatened by each hazard.

HEALTH:

1. The labs pumus pan is used all day long and does not get cleaned at the end of the day. It hasn't been cleaned in the last month.
2. Hand pieces are only autoclaved if they have blood on them.
3. Doctor only wears gloves when doing surgery. Other employees wear face shields but are not allowed to wear face masks or lab coats because the doctor does not want the patients to feel as if they are in a dental office. He also feels that protective equipment is not necessary.
4. Coffee pot and cups for staffers is located in sterile lab.

SAFETY:

1. Lab downstairs (dentures, crowns etc) has only one exit. The windows would be very hard to get out.

10. Has this condition been brought to the attention of (Mark X in all that apply)
☒ Employer   ☐ Other Government Agency (specify)

11. Please indicate your desire
☒ Do not reveal my name to the Employer   ☐ My name may be revealed to the Employer

12. The Undersigned (Mark X in one box)
☒ Employee   ☐ Federal Safety and Health Committee   ☐ Employer
☐ Representative of Employees   ☐ Other Including Former Employees (specify)
believes that a violation of an Occupational Safety or Health standard exists which is a job safety or health hazard at the establishment named on this form.

Fig. 3–1 OSHA charges of noncompliance.

CHAPTER FOUR

---◆---

NEUROLOGY

THE ELECTRONIC DENTAL OFFICE

*"Dental success, in the twenty-first century,
will depend less upon the skillful employment of the
dental handpiece than upon the prudent
deployment of the computer."*

—DUANE A. SCHMIDT, PREDICTION

Read my blips! I won't blow you away with computerese. Two reasons: I don't speak the language, and we don't need to understand computer hardware to get along with computer software. That said, what do we need? Let's start back in the twentieth century.

Once upon a time, back in the late 1900s, the traditional front desk was where all the business activity for the practice took place. There patients were greeted, phone calls were received, payments received, appointments made, and insurance forms, statements, and letters created, mailed, and stored.

It sort of had to be that way because the appointment book lolled over several square feet of desk, the one-write ledger system hid additional counter space, file cabinets cluttered the room, and that's where the telephone and typewriter squatted. Space was at such a premium in those cramped quarters that room for a credit card machine, document copier, and fax was out of the question.

That homey little business reception area was also an endearing place where everyone assembled; lines formed; gossip reigned; charts, time, and tempers all got frayed or lost; and people were treated like numbers.

The computer changed all that. Now that we're into twenty-first century dentistry, the office command center can be anywhere AT&T hooks up. Those initials refer to two things: Both the telephone company and A Telephone & Terminal. It is not inconceivable that a phone booth could be a viable reception desk, and the booth could be miles from the office.

Before you dismiss these revelations to be the ranting of a senile old fossil (I admit to two out of three), consider that this concept is proven in dentistry. We do it at Gentle Dental, every day.

We call it the Electronic Dental Office, which I shorten to EDO. Early-day dentist visionaries foresaw a "paperless" dental office. Twenty years ago we set out to do more than talk about it. We simply did it. Funny thing. Now that we're there, we've learned that there is somewhere else. The destination once again has proven to be a journey. What a trip it is!

The goal is to improve the quality of the dental experience through the intelligent use of smart machines (Fig. 4–1).

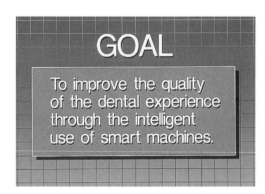

Fig. 4-1

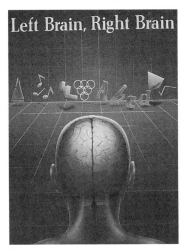

Fig. 4–2

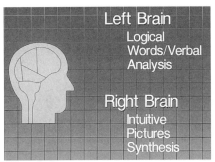

Fig. 4–3

Left Brain
Logical
Words/Verbal
Analysis

Right Brain
Intuitive
Pictures
Synthesis

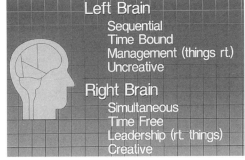

Fig. 4–4

Left Brain
Sequential
Time Bound
Management (things rt.)
Uncreative

Right Brain
Simultaneous
Time Free
Leadership (rt. things)
Creative

LEFT BRAIN
Creates a
Systems-Driven
Practice

General Ledger	Billing
EMC	Payroll
Job Scheduler	A/R

Fig. 4–5

RIGHT BRAIN
Creates a Patient-Sensitive Practice

Word Processing	Referral Tracker
Scheduler	Motivated Recalls
Treatment Planner	Internal Marketing

Fig. 4–6

Your Computer Choice
Demands Leadership

Booting Up
Requires Management

Fig. 4–7

Figs. 4–2 through 4–7
Explaining computers through the analogy of right brain/left brain.

The Right-Brain, Left-Brain Theory

In the early 1800s, Dr. Marc Dax, a physician in southern France, observed that patients with damage to the right side of the brain exhibited certain symptoms. He noted that patients with damage to the other side of the brain showed quite different symptoms. Based on these observations, he theorized that the two hemispheres of the brain controlled different functions.

Unfortunately, Dr. Dax died before his theory became accepted, though he had read a paper on it at his local medical society meeting. His son, however, became a physician and set out to popularize his father's theorem. Today, the theory of brain dominance, much like Dr. Dax deduced, has achieved universal acceptance.

Some fascinating books on the subject await reading at your local library, but, in a capsule, the theory states that the left brain controls logical thought, verbalization, and analysis. The right brain is intuitive, deals in pictures, and synthesizes data.

Now what does that mean? The left brain is time-bound, uncreative, and sees that things get done right. The accountant, lawyer, and scientist within you represent left-brained people.

The right brain performs simultaneous functions, because it is not time-bound. This hemisphere creates and sees that the right things get done. The entrepreneur, artist, writer, and cosmetic dentist in you function more from the right brain than the left. This explanation is brief and simplistic, but adequate to understand applications to a computer.

In Chapter One, the brain and computer were shown to have some like functions. This right-brain, left-brain capacity is again analogous. Think of the hemispheres of the brain and the dual nature of a computer this way: The left brain counts the "beans" and the right brain produces "beans" to count (Figs. 4–2 through 4–7).

Left-Brain Dental Office Functions

The first dental computer applications were completely left-brained. They were billing roles, inputting charges, keeping track of payments and patient balances, and preparing statements. That's logical because this is a left-brained world of words, measurements, and logic.

In the mid-1970s, our computer service bureau performed those strictly bean-counting functions for us. They kept track of accounts receivable and sent office statements. What an incredible burden to lift from the staff.

I still recall my disbelief when I was handed that first amazing aging of accounts receivable. Holding that document, I felt the power this awesome thing called a computer held, and at once, the switch turned on in my quest for the EDO.

Bean-counting computer functions in dentistry have expanded, until today they include, not only billing and accounts receivable, but payroll, electronic insurance claims processing, general ledger, and payables. These crucial applications free staff from time-wrecking, labor-intensive, mistake-prone number pushing.

Management records are generated from these documents, giving us the tools to oversee, detect, and inspect aspects of dental practice we formerly accessed only through other labor-intensive actions. The best way to hide data in a dental office is to simply require a great deal of hand-tooling to accomplish the job. The work may get done the first time, but never the second. End of discussion.

A further left-brain role is to automate certain scheduled activities. During the night, our system goes on alert and performs a menu of jobs we have given it. When staff arrive the next morning, either hard-copy printouts or saved internal files hold the requested findings.

Left-brain dental computer functions are first on the startup menu for dentists just launching their own computer generation. Look at it this way. An orthodontist, an oral surgeon, and a periodontist all prepared and placed a buccal pit restoration long before they got into prognathism, horizontal bony impactions, and flap surgery.

It is simply doing things in the proper order. Dentists who want the "bells and whistles" of dental computers—right-brain functions, networking, Computerized Dental Radiography, charting—must walk with left-brain functions first, or they will increase manyfold their odds of failure. Houses, and dental computer systems, are built on a foundation. No one shingles the roof on a structure with a crumbling foundation.

Left-brain dental computer functions are systems-driven. That is, they are mechanical and dependent on rote methods, employed over and over again. On the other side, right-brain dental computer functions are patient driven. That is, they depend on patient factors to trigger their need. Here's what I mean by that.

RIGHT-BRAIN DENTAL
OFFICE FUNCTIONS

Right-brain dental computer functions swept on the scene decades after left-brain aspects were purring right along. These attributes add the clinical dimension to our systems. Be careful, however, that you do not drive down the freeway at 80 miles an hour, backward. You will head for serious trouble.

So it is with dentists who want to perform clinical charting, for example, and it isn't integrated (networked) into their left-brain systems of ledger notes, patient charts, and billing systems. Remember the quote that led off Chapter Two? Think of the computer system as a body composed of many parts, none more important than another.

Those who wish to sell you an eye (an intraoral camera) as a stand-alone, or a mouth (tooth and periodontal charting), or an ear (computerized dental X-rays) as stand-alone systems, do not have your total interests at heart. Dental systems must network. That is, they must work in concert for this body of computerized functions to make sense.

Would it make sense to buy a stand-alone braking system for your auto, if it did not work with the rest of the parts? Would a sensible dentist set up an air system that worked in air syringes but wouldn't propel an air turbine? Would you wire your office with voltages that worked with some electrical parts and failed with others? Of course not. Then think no differently about computerized parts.

Not only must dental parts network, they must be *able* to network. This facet and feature may be more difficult for us computer laypersons to assess. Difficult doesn't equal impossible. We'll study more parameters as we go, and when we reach the end of the book, you will know all you need to know to assess either your first or your next dental computer system.

CLINICAL NOTES

Right-brain dental computer functions include clinical notes. These are blocks of text, input with a keystroke. The principal reason this text should be input to a patient's chart is to preserve a record of events occurring before, during, or after an appointment.

The text provides legal protection for the doctor and may give clues to further treatment, should that be needed. For example, prior to a simple extraction, a block of text may be input with two keystrokes, T and E. Note that items to be added are all on the left side of the block of data, for ease of entering the numbers. The text notes:

> TE: _____ B/P, _____ Temp., pt. ambulatory, alert and in apparent good health, presurgery consent video shown, all questions answered regarding informed consent and informed consent signed, patient stating he felt well and that he could tolerate the procedure.

> _____ Carpules of Marcaine with 1/200k epi, tooth extracted via elevator and forceps technique, minimal blood loss, no complications, post-op instructions, pt. told to return to office PRN.

Given today's litigious climate, the ways this block of text protects the doctor and office are apparent. Few would disagree with the concept of entering this information in a patient's record. Every word builds further barriers to thwart litigation.

Consider having to write out this entire text, prior to each surgery. Would it get done every time? Maybe. Can an office afford the staff time that it would take to write out this message? Possibly not. Could it be forgotten? Probably.

In the flurry of a packed practice, a written message may become abbreviated to the point that it may not record essential data. In the bustle of a busy day, the message may be put off ("I'll catch up on these charts, later"), and later may never arrive. Either abbreviating the message to insignificance or "forgetting" to record it creates a dangerous exposure for the office.

Our staff opens the clinical note file, then inputs that statement with these exact keystrokes: T and E. That's two letters only, and the letters stand for Tooth Extraction. Therefore the code that prints the entire block of data cannot be forgotten. Since there are blanks that must be filled in, the note reminds staff, for example, to be certain to take vital signs, prior to all surgeries, and record carpule usage following surgery.

The time it takes to type TE is one second. The time it takes to write out the same data is a couple of minutes. Could even a fragment of doubt exist about which is the safer, better, quicker, cheaper, easier, faster, or more prudent way to input clinical data?

Periodontal concerns are the latest legal fad. Suing a dentist for a lifetime of a patient's own neglect has led to some ridiculous awards for equally ludicrous claims. Yet, they exist. Refer back to the ADA statement on OSHA claims: All claims must be defended, even scurrilous ones.

Hygienists often consume the entire appointment time doing the things they must: Scale, polish, treat, and entreat their patients, plus teach and reteach about home care, reappoint, and escort the patient to the receptionist. Charting can become rote, minimal, assumed, and inadequate, given the demands on hygienists' time. Here is a typical hygiene clinical note we employ for a Routine Prophy, R3 (which means a three-month recall):

> R3: Routine hand scale, polish, and floss. Minimal plaque and calculus, healthy gingiva, resilient tissue, pink color. Reviewed home care: Brushing and flossing. Discussed periodontal disease, etiology, progression, and treatment. Showed periodontal chart. Recommended three month recall to maintain dental health. Patient understood information given; all questions answered.

This periodontal clinical note is the same for four, six, and twelve months, depending upon the circumstance. The note takes two keys to enter, P3 (or P4 or P6). It is difficult to forget that P3 means a *prophy* at *three* months.

Another periodontal clinical note enters data from a periodontal scaling in this fashion:

> PS:__(A lead-off blank line for personalized data)_____. Ultrasonic scale; heavy plaque and calculus. Discussed presence of periodontal disease. Explained periodontal disease, etiology, progression, and treatment. Showed periodontal charting. Discussed appropriate home care, reviewed brushing and flossing. Explained need for additional cleanings and appointments. Patient understood information given; all questions answered.

A clinical note for a bridge preparation will start with the two-letter code BP.

> BP: _____ Carpules of 2% lido with 1/100k epi., prep completed for gold/MB bridge, retraction cord, impression with Impergum, temp fabricated and cemented with temp cement, checked occl. and margins, pt. advised to return to office if any problems with temp. occur, that gum tissues may be sore, and tooth may be thermally sensitive while wearing temp.

The question that bears answering—if your staff does not input notes as complete as these—what will your defense be, when you are sued for failing to provide full-scale periodontal salvation? Someone *will* claim you failed. The *only* question is what will be your answer?

Note how easily this simple, unforgettable, one-second keystroke enters blocks of data that could be critical in a defense of periodontal malpractice. Naturally, the suit will be aimed not at the hygienist but at the doctor and the office.

A clinical note for a crown seat is triggered by the simple code keystroke CR. Giving these and other functions simple names or codes ensures the likelihood of not forgetting them, thus their being readily used. In computer lingo this is called being "user-friendly."

> CR: ___ Carpules of 2% lido with 1/100k epi., removed temp., cleaned tooth of residual temp. cement, seated crown and checked occl., margins and proximal contacts, cemented crown with ZnPO4 cement, rechecked occl., margins and proximal contacts, cleaned tooth of residual cement, pt. told to contact office PRN if problems arise with crown.

In the years before we accessed this resource of keystroke clinical notes, we kept notes the old-fashioned way. We thought they were pretty good notes, too. The deficiencies of those notes didn't surface until my trial, one more time that I banged into the wall going down the dental hallway of life.

My patient had refused post-op appointments and an interstitial cellulitis developed. He was hospitalized and required oral surgery to drain the spaces. Photos of him in the hospital, that his family fortuitously took while he was there, were shown to the jury to illustrate the "damage" I had done.

Further, according to his counsel, Jeffers probably had a general infection and illness that—had I taken his temperature—would have precluded surgery that day. Therefore, the jury assumed that I was imprudent by extracting teeth on a man who, in his attorney's view, had serious infection.

The fact that we had ruled out precluding causes on the day of surgery, and had taken his temperature—which was normal and NOT recorded, could not be substantiated in the trial. Two lessons I learned were: 1. Never go to trial if the insurance company will pay off, up front and 2. One cannot record too many ledger notes. There are no alternatives.

After a week's trial, during which time my attorney assured me there was no way the jury could find me guilty, I was judged to bear 90 percent of the blame for his distress. Fair? What we think about it doesn't matter. The jury believed his story and awarded him $80,000 (Fig. 4–8).

Naturally, the insuror paid for it, but if you think that ends the cost, think again. From that date on, the insuror refused new insurance. I had to buy insurance with a $5,000 deductible—meaning I pay the first $5,000 of *defense* costs, not *awards* costs that may be rendered—and my liability insurance premiums soared by 500 percent. The incident must be reported to the Board of Dental Examiners, and I live with this stain on my record forever. There's no going back to redo or retry the case.

KEYSTROKE INPUTS

The term "keystroke" may need definition. People newly acquainted with a computer are often overawed by how this electrical machine does its tricks so rapidly. They fail to realize that a computer is nothing more than a bunch of switches that turn things on and turn other things off.

A computer also can be programmed to ask "What if?" and then respond accordingly. *That is, if I want to italicize this sentence, I can do so by pushing some buttons.* I can highlight the sentence, then push the pair of *italicize* keys and instantly the sentence is italicized. Since I only highlighted this single sentence, when the italics arrive at the end of the

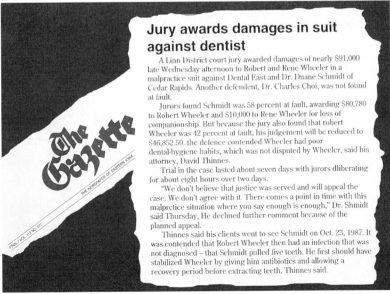

Jury awards damages in suit against dentist

A Linn District court jury awarded damages of nearly $91,000 late Wednesday afternoon to Robert and Rene Wheeler in a malpractice suit against Dental East and Dr. Duane Schmidt of Cedar Rapids. Another defendent, Dr. Charles Choi, was not found at fault.

Jurors found Schmidt was 58 percent at fault, awarding $80,780 to Robert Wheeler and $10,000 to Rene Wheeler for loss of companionship. But because the jury also found that robert Wheeler was 42 percent at fault, his judgement will be reduced to $46,852.50. the defence contended Wheeler had poor dental-hygiene habits, which was not disputed by Wheeler, said his attorney, David Thinnes.

Trial in the case lasted about seven days with jurors dliberating for about eight hours over two days.

"We don't believe that justice was served and will appeal the case. We don't agree with it. There comes a point in time with this malprctice situation where you say enough is enough," Dr. Shmidt said Thursday. He declined further comment because of the planned appeal.

Thinnes said his clients went to see Schmidt on Oct. 23, 1987. It was contended that Robert Wheeler then had an infection that was not diagnosed – that Schmidt pulled five teeth. He first should have stabilized Wheeler by giving him antibiotics and allowing a recovery period before extracting teeth, Thinnes said.

Fig. 4–8 News clipping of the Jeffers trial.

sentence, it is told, "When you get to the end of the highlighted sentence, stop." It stops on command.

Programs are merely series of many commands, covering all the "what ifs" that could occur. Indeed they are awesome. To be sure, they happen at the speed of light. But when we learn the right switches, and have a computer containing the correct programs, we achieve incredible results.

For example, my typing skills are confined to two fingers, the first finger of my left hand and the middle finger of my right hand—I lost a fingertip as a teen. Yet, I will easily type every one of the 50,000 or so words in this book on my Compaq, Contura 410CX, portable laptop. This word-processing program goes by the name WordPerfect (WP). If I can do it, anyone can.

The label "keystroke" may mean a single key, a pair of keys depressed one after the other (like the TE command just noted) or a pair of keys, depressed together. Liken a pair of keys to the shift key on a typewriter, which is depressed while another key is hit to obtain a capital letter.

I almost wish it were more complex than that, but it isn't. Many pseudo-intellectuals would have you believe in a computer mystique. Balderdash, or some such phrase. Computer keys are simply electrical switches with funny names. Instead of "on" and "off," like an honest switch should be named, they read with cyber-names like F1, F2, Enter, Home, End, Pg Up, or Esc.

Why talk computer mechanics to dentists? There are three commanding reasons:

1. **Some dentists have no computers.** Fearing the technology, they have not yet availed their practice of the computer dimension in dentistry.

2. **Many dentists are computer-illiterate.** Being unable to access their own computer, they leave operational decisions to staff.

3. **Most dentists use but a third of available computer functions.** Even though they can access their own system, they refuse to learn its true potential and limp along on limited opportunity.

If we assume that a prudent practice should never consider operations without utilizing computer technology, then those three excuses reach critical mass. The example about clinical notes is merely one of a series of arguments I will advance to convince you to:

1. Become computer literate,

2. Be the decision-maker to decide the depth of computer technology in your office, and

3. Expand your horizons to employ more advanced computer programs.

In the computer beginning, it was acceptable for staff to choose, install, and implement the computer. That was because the only computer options a dentist had were left-brained choices. Billing functions are rarely engaged in by dentists.

When right-brained choices came along, computer-illiterate dentists found they didn't know how to employ this new monster. If you don't know how to swim, why get scuba diving gear? If you can't sky-dive, why own a parachute?

Today's dentist is faced with new computer choices. Right-brained functions require dentist decisions, and we cannot give away our trust. The right brain of the computer involves the dentist as never before, and this is where the profession heads. Colleagues, it is time to get involved. I'll help you get there.

Right-brain computer options include word processing, scheduling, referral tracking, recall systems, treatment planning, and internal marketing. Just as staff can neither diagnose nor prescribe a treatment plan, they cannot decide what parts of clinical (right-brain) computer usage should be booted up.

A mediocre system in a well-managed practice will do better than a fine system in a poorly managed practice.

WORD PROCESSING

Word processing (w-p) goes beyond writing books, an exercise understandably few people wish to agonize over. In the office, w-p means communication with staff members and communication with patients.

Staff notices keep staff informed of changes in office philosophy, new or renewed emphasis, refreshment of old rules, and a recall to teamwork. Properly conceived, staff notices are the pacemaker that keeps the staff heart pumping evenly and productively.

The staff mission manual also springs from the w-p aspect of our computers. Here we engage staff members in codifying their job descriptions, defining how to do their various jobs, and discuss goals. This manual becomes the training manual for new employees and a retraining manual for existing staff.

W-p communicates with patients through the U.S. Postal Service. Using formatted letters, personalized letters go to new patients to welcome them to the practice, to thank referring patients, and thank referring colleagues. Letters also leave the office daily to refer a patient to a specialist, to request collection, and to market services to select niche markets.

A dental office can function without communication with staff and with patients, but not for long. A dental office can function without nitrous oxide. A dental office can function without a typewriter. A dental office can function without treating endodontic, pedodontic, prosthetic, periodontic, and oral surgical needs. But why? Why should any office penalize itself in the communications age and fail to avail itself of resources readily and virtually at our fingertips? I have no idea.

When I began dentistry, I visited the office of a gentleman dentist who practiced using a gorgeous walnut chair, upholstered in red velvet fabric. I would give a lot to have that chair today. In the corner stood an imposing open cathode-ray-tube X-ray. He functioned, but he couldn't compete, nor could he keep pace with the new era that I watched dawn in dentistry.

Dentists who deny that right-brain computer concepts are essentials, not frills, are practicing—for all intents and purposes—with red velvet chairs, with open cathode-ray X-ray tubes. They won't be around very long. We, the competition, will leave them in the dust.

SCHEDULER

"I've only got my schedule and the hygienist's, so there is no need to get involved with a scheduler on a computer." That's certainly a valid view. However, employing a scheduler goes beyond the simple concept of ridding the office of the appointment book(s). Here's why.

Consider two methods of learning: vertical and lateral. Say you want to speed up sending 300 statements each month. Your computer specialist advises a program that saves four hours of labor, and you wax ecstatic. That solution approaches the problem vertically, just as a dental office with its own dental laboratory has vertically integrated its business.

By speeding up sending statements, you do the same thing, only do it better, quicker, cheaper, or easier. Those are salutary benefits, not to be sneezed at. No one kicks those savings out the door, but consider that there might be another approach to the same problem.

You tell your management consultant that you want to send 300 statements faster each month. The consultant suggests improving financial and treatment planning to reduce the number of statements to 150 each month, then suggests that statements be sent twice a month. Suddenly cash flow soars.

The latter approach represents lateral thinking. Instead of solving the problem by doing the same thing, the same way only better, the solution rests in stepping to the side of the problem and rethinking how to solve it. In this instance, a new solution saves far more than the obvious computer solution of high-speeding statement preparation.

Consider the acceptance of credit cards. Traditionally you call the credit card company for approval, make an imprint of the card, fill out the ticket, have the patient sign the ticket, and batch and send the vendor copies at the end of the day, and the card company sends you a check. That's really a wonderful deal, as far as it goes. I can recall practicing before there were credit cards, and life was not as easy.

What if . . . you purchase a small device that allows you to swipe the card through it? In seconds, without human intervention, credit approval comes through, the ticket rolls out of a small printer, the patient signs it, and the money is in your office account within 48 hours, without batching and sending a hard copy to the credit card company.

That approach reduces a problem by vertically integrating a solution into the practice. The time, labor, and dollar float savings are enormous. Saved time can be better spent by staff working with patients than by staff working with systems.

A still better way to solve financing is to prepare treatment and financial plans that obviate the need for credit cards. Perhaps the office offers an interest-free payment plan. Would that help solve some financing problems for some patients? It does for some people we serve in our office.

Here's how we developed our interest-free payment plan. We went to a branch office of a national loan company. They were eager for new business and we settled on these terms: We would offer an interest-free payment plan, dividing the total by 12 monthly payments. We would fax them an application, using their forms, and they would give approval or denial within 24 hours.

The total had to be more than $200. They discounted the payment to us at 10 percent, without recourse. That is, if the patient failed to make a payment, the loan company couldn't come back to us. That's all there was to setting it up.

When people say they don't want to use a credit card because of the interest on the unpaid balance, or the card is full and denied, we simply switch over to the loan company and offer an interest-free loan. If the loan company denies them, we do not offer another option except prepayment.

There is one feature unknowing computer salespersons tout that should never be mentioned. That is the ability of the computer software to make payment booklets, so the patient can make regular payments to the dental office. Yes, and the tooth fairy leaves silver dollars.

We are a dental office, not a loan company. If a credit card company, a loan company, and a bank refuse this person credit, why should we be so naive as to think we can outguess the professionals? GD offers six forms of deferred payment: MasterCard, Visa, American Express, Discover, an interest-free loan, and a prepayment plan. That's enough. Most businesses don't offer that many.

When your patient demands to make payments to you, rather than to a credit card company or your loan company, seize the offer. There is only one kicker. He or she must pay ahead of time, and when the patient has made payments sufficient to receive the crown or denture, for example, then the paid prosthesis is delivered. We even give him our 5 percent discount that we offer for payment on the day of service. It's okay to print a payment book for this person.

Some people advise scrapping the word *discount* and substituting the word *courtesy*. I don't see anything wrong with that except one thing.

Using a foreign word, or a term in a new and unfamiliar manner, creates a mental barrier. Example: Obfuscation is never justification.

While you know the meaning of those words, you had to stop and translate, to figure out what I said. A communicator tries for the easiest language to say what's on his or her mind. Dental offices should, too.

The word courtesy is a barrier, because people must translate what in the world you are trying to say. No one misunderstands or needs to translate the word discount. Discount works, so my advice is to use what works.

We've strayed from the scheduler, but not as much as you think. The reason for this aside was to emphasize that the purpose of the scheduler is not to vertically solve scheduling problems, but to laterally resolve them. Yes, making appointments on a scheduler is faster. Any reasonably proficient staff can pick it up in hours.

The lateral solution to appointing comes when the chairside assistants, freed from having to find the appointment book, can suddenly make appointments at the chair, at an operatory monitor and keyboard. While an anesthetic becomes profound, while a cement or impression material sets, while waiting for doctor, the chairside assistant can make the next appointment, without even talking to the front desk.

There's another situation where this saves time, effort, and money. Say the phone is ringing off the hook and the receptionist is going crazy. Another business person at the office answers the phone. Like the chairside assistant, she has a terminal before her, so that she can make an appointment or pull up a ledger to answer a question.

Perhaps a patient wants a specific time period for an appointment —the scheduler simply finds those times. Maybe the patient wants to appoint with doctor and the hygienist, in concert. The scheduler does so. Possibly the patient wants a specific chairside assistant, and the scheduler responds in kind.

The benefits of the scheduler go beyond vertically doing something better and faster. They involve new methods of operation. New dimensions may easily translate into new opportunities to change the way you see your patients, but, more importantly, they may change the way your patients see you.

REFERRAL TRACKER

The computer's right brain keeps a mountain of data within it and can combine it in so many interesting ways. One good management way is the referral tracker, a tool that tells you how many patients came to your office from various resources, an important number to know. There is another number even more important. That number is the dollar volume produced from referred patients.

Take, for example, referrals from two sources. Studying your tracker, you note that physician referrals amount to only 12 patients during a period of time. The time can be your choice as the referral tracker will list referrals by month. You also note that during the same period of time you received 24 referrals from a newspaper ad.

On the surface it seems as though you should concentrate on newspaper display ads, over focusing on physicians. Except that you look to the next column of numbers on the referral tracker and discover that newspaper referrals produced $3,000 worth of business, while the physician referrals produced $7,000 worth of business. Hmmm, you say, this takes some thinking. At least you have hard data to think about.

If the newspaper ad only cost $300, the return on investment was all right. Don't stop it. Maybe change its focus to attract more of the business you want, such as cosmetic, prosthetic, pedodontic, or whatever. Then focus your marketing muscle on physicians, your source of higher-quality patients or, at least, patients who have greater needs.

Join a hospital staff, give a talk at a medical meeting, make a mailing, or offer a spiff of some sort to the physicians, maybe a preferred discount to their staff. Like my business friend, Ed, always said, "Let's do something, Schmidty, even if it's wrong." Sometimes that can be sound advice.

RECALL

A motivated recall program is a key aspect of the kind of dental management software you want to live with. You need to bring up lists of recall patients to work with in various manners. You will want to mail patients, on continuous-form postcards, reminders that they are due for a recall, or have an appointment made and need to call and confirm.

You may want to launch a calling program, utilizing hygiene downtime, or hire a senior who perhaps once worked in a dental office and can talk some of the language to make confirmation calls. Of course, the hygiene list shows conditions that the hygienist or doctor has noted which require close watching and therefore reminding.

If your system is truly alert—that is, has the right software—you will provide a headset for the callers and pull up a calling list on the screen. This awards the caller the convenience of calling patients at home or office with a keystroke, H for home, O for office. The benefits of time saved, efficiency gained, and full hygiene chairs are immeasurable.

The next generation of callers will be the system itself, calling and confirming every appointment, every day, without human intervention. Too impersonal? Decidedly, if we are talking the 1970s. Too impersonal for the 21st century? Not even remotely so.

TREATMENT PLAN

No right-brain advantage is more powerful than the ability to create printed, accurate, easy-to-understand treatment plans (TP). There's a bit of a left brain here, in that the TP dishes out a lot of numbers, such as cost of each procedure, divided into patient portion and insurance portion. The way we use those numbers to inform our patients is right-brained.

Studies have reported that more than half the problems of communication between patients and their dentist relate to failure to be informed of costs. When TPs become the office standard, that barrier is blown away. Here's how we work the program.

The doctor examines the patient and conceives a diagnosis. The assistant constructs a chart on screen and then formats a TP, based on the doctor's diagnosis. From the beginning of TP formulation until it is printed, no more than a few minutes elapse.

The TP contains the procedures to be performed, costs, insurance breakdown, and the number of appointments and approximate time required for each appointment. For example, the first appointment may be for a buildup, prep, and impression, requiring 90 minutes. A cost breakdown is provided for this appointment.

Support documents are also printed, which explain the terms of the TP. That is, it will be honored for a specified period of time (your choice, ours is three months). The words are defined, since lay persons may not know what a buildup, prep, impression, temp, and seat mean.

Terms of payment are also defined in the support paragraphs, telling the office requirement of 50 percent down on the day of prep and 50 percent at the seat appointment. Deferred payment methods are noted. (MasterCard, Visa, American Express, Discover and the interest-free plan, prepayment are always an option.)

Once the plan is printed, a few keystrokes assemble the data in moments, and a laser printer produces a clean copy. The chairside assistant reviews the TP with the patient. She tells what will occur during each appointment, how long the sessions will last, what costs are involved, when payments are due, and answers the patient's questions.

Most patient questions are answered better by the assistant than the doctor, for the assistant and the patient often relate better without the doctor's presence. Should questions arise that require the dentist to answer, he or she is brought into the discussion for the answer.

The TP requires that financial arrangements acceptable to the office are properly conducted according to office protocol. We'll study those later. The chairside assistant makes the initial appointment, bearing in mind that every day of delay between today and the starting day lessens the odds of TP fulfillment.

After careful study of all state laws governing permissible dental-assisting duties, it is a pleasure to announce that: In every state it is legal for dental assistants to talk!

Dental assistants do an incredible job making these presentations and will sell more dentistry than any dentist I know. People rise to the level of expectation, just as many people grow into a challenging job. Assistants who have personality and moxie will accept the role of explainer and perform the job magnificently.

Dentists who fail to challenge their staff with important roles will find their team has a hard time getting up much steam or team spirit. Assigning them useful roles beyond mechanical duties shows them how much you respect them and their ability to make the office succeed.

The method we use is the chairside assistant presentation, on the spot, the day of examination and diagnosis. Some dentists reappoint for presentations that are complex and probably not nearly as successful as they would believe.

In my pedodontist life, I fashioned a beautiful sales message to sell a space maintainer. In those days, pedodontists had few big-ticket items in our menu of tricks. There were no sealants, fluoride treatments or composites, just fillings, stainless steel crowns, and space maintainers.

Wanting desperately to sell space maintainers, I created a practiced, 20-minute lecture that was beautiful, if unsuccessful. As I spoke of mesial-axial inclinations, and mesial molar drift from deciduous tooth loss, the mother gazed at me with waxen eyes. She was oblivious to what I was saying, unable to understand anything past the first hard word that hung her up.

When I finished, I proudly asked if we could start this needed procedure. Her reply was pretty standard, "I'll have to ask his father." She hadn't the foggiest notion of what to ask the child's father, but it stalled me off. They left and rarely reappointed for the spacer.

As time went by, I got busy, despite myself—not because of my oratorical brilliance. The busier I got, the fewer 20-minute segments were available for spacer presentations. The speech kept getting shorter and shorter—about like clinical notes in a busy practice that does not have keystroke entry capability. As the speech wound down, I made an amazing discovery: I sold more spacers when I said less! What an ego-buster that finding was, but what great news to learn.

The speech came down from 20 minutes to 20 seconds. It went, "Mrs. Jones, Betty has lost this baby tooth too soon. While we wait for the new tooth to come in—which will be around fifth grade in school— her jaw is going to shrink, unless I prop the space open. We call it a spacer and this is what one looks like. It costs this much. Shall we do that for Betty?"

Twenty understandable seconds of English and the sale occurs now. After giving a few hundred spacer talks, I decided staff could do it as well, or better, than I. They could and did. From then on, I was saved endless repetition, as staff gave me my first lesson in learning to respect other's full capabilities.

EXTERNAL AND INTERNAL MARKETING

External marketing delivers new patients across the office threshold. Here I group: signs, Yellow Pages, Time & Temperature, Doctors With A Heart, newspaper ads, and our Thanksgiving Day dinner for seniors.

Internal marketing bonds patients to our practice and fires them up to refer us new patients. Here I list: office ambience, office brochure, patient care forms, letters, the EDO and, as we have already discussed, staff attitudes and the recall system.

Oddly enough, I have no goof to relate about my external marketing. No reprimand, lawsuit, or peer review about our advertising. I suppose that's because, despite the local GD high profile, we have never resorted to hype or hyperbole, nor have we made excessive or exaggerated claims. We've merely told the truth.

Why does someone call our office over dozens of other dental offices they could call? This is a key question. If we can find the reason, then market to it, we may open the doors to all the new business we can handle.

An old professional organization pamphlet once proclaimed several ways to find a new dentist. The first was to call your local dental college. I think that's fair. However, I graduated from dental college before most of the current professors were born. Will they—who have never set foot inside the walls of my office—be able to fairly evaluate and recommend my services? No, I think not.

Another was to call your medical doctor or pharmacist, and ask who is a good dentist. Really? Those colleagues both believe the mouth is a fine place to put a thermometer or to pop a pill. What do they know about good dental health or good dental service?

Another idea listed was to ask your neighbor, friend, or coworker who they would suggest to be a good dentist. Once more, these are completely subjective opinions. Is it possible that a neighbor understands how to evaluate the scientific skills of a dentist? That is truly doubtful.

After reading this pamphlet, one concludes that there simply is no fair way to find a good dentist. That shouldn't surprise us, because we make many major decisions in life on skimpy evidence. For example, take three of the most important decisions of your life—your choice of career, community, and cohabitant. Did you make any of those decisions on the basis of logic? If you did, you are alone in the world.

Career? Is dentistry the only profession in which you could have succeeded? Community? Is your locale the only one that would have supported you? Cohabitant? Was your arrangement "made in heaven," or is it barely possible someone other than your current significant other could have fulfilled your life?

People choose to visit our office on the basis of emotional bias, supported by whatever logic makes them feel comfortable. They may have heard we are gentle, or believe we are because we have named ourselves that. They may have heard that the dollar goes further in our office than perhaps others. They may want hours when other offices are closed. They may want to be seen promptly, and have gotten the runaround elsewhere. They may want nitrous oxide, payment plans, someone who speaks German, a dentist who won't excoriate them for having not seen a dentist for years, or someone with a large, free parking lot.

People do not choose a dentist on sound, logical pretexts for the same reason they do not choose their career, community, and mate on the basis of sound, logical rationale. They choose on emotional bias, and we do well to present them with a broad scope of reasons to choose us.

Since we are educated beings—schooled in science and logic—we reject the thought that people choose a dentist for such simple reasons. After we reject that thought, we drive across town to buy a case of refreshments, because the price is a dollar under the local grocers'. Go figure.

If you do not believe people choose dentists for simplistic reasons, then you give people more credit than they deserve. People do not make logical life choices. Turn on television and watch infomercials that present sales pitches to cheering audiences who applaud the fact that this blender/aerator/smoker (worth at least $3) can be bought for a mere $14.99, every month for the next quarter. Consider what situation comedies are most popular and wonder if you would—or why you do—watch them.

Watch wrestling on television and wonder who else is watching. Some of the people watching will be the ones who call tomorrow with a dental problem. Never, ever overestimate the intelligence of the American population. Please don't misunderstand. None of this is said in derogation. I say this only in an attempt to bring your thinking to where the real world lives.

If we apply to socioeconomics the normal distribution curve we learned in college, we know there are wealthy people and paupers, yet most of us live in the middle of the curve. I call it the mainstream of dentistry, the niche market our office aims for.

This is the largest market, the backbone of America. These people watch wrestling. They watch infomercials and situation comedies. They pay their bills. They raise their families. They go to church. They punch time clocks. They have dental insurance. They are wonderful human beings.

Failed cultures from time immemorial crashed because they did not have a strong middle class. It is these people in the middle of the normal distribution curve who distinguish America from almost every other culture in history. Thank God we are them.

Yet there is a cultural snobbishness apparent in American dentistry that doesn't work to the advantage of this profession. I'm old enough to say it, and so I will. I sorrow to see dentists target the cultural elite as patients, at the expense of the vast middle class.

Recently, we called every dental office in our city and asked if they would take a welfare patient. Only one-third would accept a welfare patient and, of those, many said it would take as long as three weeks to get in. What's going on? Unless dentistry in America changes its priority system, we are headed for cataclysmic changes that will be brought about by a populace unserved. We are better than that.

GD external marketing begins with signs. In the late 1950s, the ADA Rules of Ethics declared that dental signs could boast lettering no larger than six inches tall. Never, in my greatest imaginings, could I have envisioned a day when a thousand-pound, lighted, 30-foot GD sign would command attention on a major highway, outside my office (Figs. 4–9, 4–10).

Our referral tracker reports some people become our new patients because of our sign. If I didn't know it was true, I would doubt that statement. Strange as the thought of choosing a dentist on the basis of his sign is, we gladly accept and serve patients no matter how they find us. I would accept them just as quickly if they came to us because I was their son's Scoutmaster, sang next to them in the church choir, or worked with them on a charity drive. Is there much of a difference?

A word of caution about reports of referral sources. Often what people may say masks the truth. Their inability to recall may be well-intentioned. For example, new patients may say that it was the GD Yellow Pages ad that brought them in.

In a sense they may be correct, but in another sense, it was more likely a coworker who recommended us. The patient did not remember that, last year, the guy on the next workbench told him how pleased he had been during his visit to Gentle Dental. Later, when a dental need arose, he looked us up in the phone book, and our ad triggered a hidden memory of his friend's endorsement.

The GD Yellow Pages ad has no "Care Bears," "We Cater to Cowards," or line drawings of dentists or toothbrushes with cute sayings on them. These ads, while seemingly clever, never draw patients to the office. They are a waste of time and money.

Put facts in your ad—the more the better. Choose the largest ad you can cram into your budget. No matter the cost, a good ad, filled with data, will draw more new patients than you believe possible. Your ad referral tracker will astound you with what a good Yellow Pages ad can produce. No one casually reads the Yellow Pages. People are in those yellowed pages for a reason, exactly the same reason you peeked in them the last time. Was it last week, or was it yesterday when you last looked?

Understanding some of the protocol of how these ads work can help your employment of this medium. The largest ad in the dentists' section is always the first ad. The largest, oldest ad—assuming two offices have the same size ad—will have the front position.

Last year another dentist bought a full-page ad, putting his ad opposite ours. I didn't want my ad diluted by facing his, so, this year, we simply took out two pages (Fig. 4–12). These pages appear face-to-face in the front of the section, pushing the competitor's ad behind us.

Time & Temperature is a service we launched about eight years ago. Local residents call a well-known number and receive a five-second message, followed by the time and the temperature. In a city of 100,000+ we receive in excess of 7,000 calls daily. These people want something we have—the time and the temperature. Our five-second ad conditions our market to hear our office name, again and again.

It is important to know what you want from each advertising venue. The Yellow Pages ad, for example, aims at three targets:

1. Newcomers with a dental need,

2. People with an emergency need, and

3. People who cannot reach their regular dentist.

Time & Temperature is a market conditioner, merely getting people to hear our name, over and again—the average Cedar Rapidian calls the service four times monthly. Newspaper display ads, in the same vein, put our name before people so when they need a dentist, they cannot forget GD.

Someone has said three out of five people are seeking a new dentist. I'm not sure the number is that high, or even if it is that low. Whatever the number, the concept is hard to dispute, given our new patient flow. Market conditioning merely positions GD to be thought of at the buying moment. That's all we ask.

Our newspaper ad simply says: "Gentle Dental, We Take Pains" (Fig. 4–11). The double entendre is intended. We will ride with this ad for decades. Why? Because we believe "We take pains" speaks volumes about our office in three little words. When you have a good slogan, ride with it.

The problem advertising agencies have with their clients is that the buyer wants too much for his money. He wants to make several marketing points, believing he gets more for his ad dollar when, in fact, he waters down his own message. An ad does less when it says too much.

The second problem advertisers have is that they want to change an ad that works. If the ad pulls customers, why change it? The reason companies often change good marketing campaigns is client boredom, not buyer saturation. That makes no sense when we consider how difficult it is to build an image of a business in today's communication age.

Our "We Take Pains" ad was designed to be placed on a billboard. It never has been, but it's ready if we think it's needed. The five-second ads on Time & Temperature are toughies because five seconds isn't time to say much of anything.

Here are some samples that we believe have been effective: "Lost fillings are found every day at Gentle Dental"; "Gentle Dental serves urgent needs twenty-four hours each day"; "From seven A.M. to eight P.M., Gentle Dental daily serves urgent dental needs."

Nearly a decade ago, I invited a dozen senior staffers to lunch for a discussion of my latest brainstorm. "What if," I asked them, "we close our cash drawer on Valentine's Day and simply open our hearts and give free dentistry to people who have no money, no job, and no welfare?"

Classy people that they are, they instantly said, "Yes, let's do it!" We began the program and it has spread across the nation under the name Doctors With A Heart (DWAH). On this day we set aside, both staff and doctors work free. We serve urgent dental needs, anything that can be performed in one appointment. The day is the finest day of practice that we enjoy all year, for each of us walks out of the office about three feet off the carpet. We generally hold a staff party that night, grateful we can give of our talents, and give something back.

While it was not intended to be a marketing promotion, simply a way of our paying community "rent," the media highlight the day on radio and television. We have many patients who laud our role in this day of free care. One patient came to us and pressed two-and-a-half dollars into my hand, saying he wanted to help us in our charity program.

At first I refused his generosity, until I was told of the circumstances. He was a well-known local street person, living homeless in the city streets. He told an assistant that he had been given five dollars for Christmas—two months earlier—and now wanted to share with others. The $2.50 was half the money he possessed on earth. Life can be humbling.

For the first several years of the program's existence, my daughter Cyd Schmidt Ferris directed the establishment of DWAH programs across the nation that copied our format. In the appendix to this book, you will find an outline of how you may start a similar program in your community.

Sixteen years ago, through a set of circumstances, I had no one to be with on Thanksgiving Day. I saw in the paper a local restaurateur was giving a free dinner to the poor so I went to his restaurant and helped bus tables. It was an incredibly enriching experience.

The next year he closed his restaurant and I determined the program should continue. I enlisted the aid of the Aging Services agency and we began a free Thanksgiving Day dinner for seniors. That first year we served 200 people. Today it has grown to more than 200 volunteers delivering more than 500 dinners to the homebound and serving another 750 in the cafeteria of a local insurance company. It wasn't planned that way, but, again, we dominate the Thanksgiving six o'clock news.

This is being written the afternoon of the dinner for this year. The fellow I just mentioned, the one who gave me half his wealth for the DWAH program, was there at the dinner. He and I have become friends. He pressed a dollar into my hand. I dared not refuse the most generous man I know. There's a story about the widow's mite in the Bible. I saw it happen in real life.

What does our external marketing cost? I don't consider the DWAH day nor the Thanksgiving dinner as costs. The Yellow Pages ad, Time & Temperature, and newspaper advertising—our three external marketing measures—probably cost less, as a percentage of gross production, than almost any other office spends.

Our budget spends less than two percent of our production for external marketing. What does this expense generate? Roughly one-third of our new business comes from external marketing, which was our goal. The other two-thirds of our new business comes from existing patients, family, and friends. This, too, is our goal.

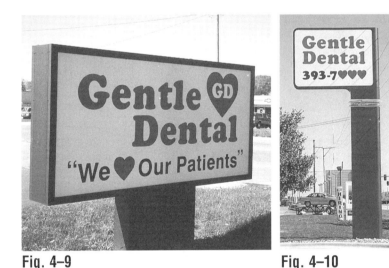

Fig. 4–9   **Fig. 4–10**

Figs. 4–9 through 4–13 Examples of external marketing.

Fig. 4–11

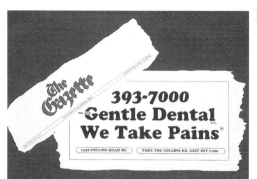

Fig. 4–12

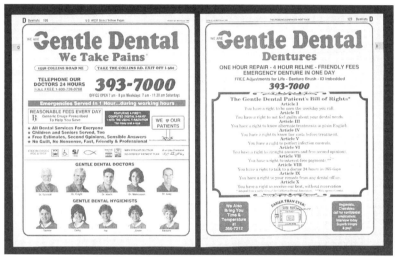

Fig. 4–13

Figs. 4–9 through 4–13 *(Continued)*

If we received our business in reversed proportions, I would seriously question our ability to deliver good dental experiences and service through internal marketing. Failing to market well internally, I would guess to be the beginning of the end. A good dental office, fulfilling its mission statement, should generate twice as many new patients from satisfied patients as from external marketing.

Dental office decor reflects the personality of its creator, just as the attitude of dental staff represents an extension of the dentist. The features we want incorporated into our dental atmosphere design are planned to please women, match the mood of our market, appear nonthreatening, present a bright, warm ambience, and contain something unique enough to make the town's gossip circuits.

In my pedodontic practice, I fashioned a circus operatory with a tented ceiling and a clown unit with air and water syringes for buttons, lions caged at the windows, and a leopard-skin covering on the pedo chair. It was the talk of the town and garnered a commanding position in pediatric dental circles in St. Albans. I learned quickly that a unique office is an enormous free ad and huge asset.

In our contemporary new office, we focused on the Iowa theme, using Iowa artists and displaying several decorations fashioned strictly for us. Nearly 60 artificial trees, bright splashes of color decor, plus a children's room featuring cartoon characters, gave our patients a lot of good "scoop."

The GD denture area is decorated in antiques and more sedate colors, and features a mid-1800s velocipede with a 54-inch front wheel and an enormous wooden hay rake. Since denture patients need not lie back, the chairs came from a beauty supply house at one-tenth the cost of a dental chair. Denture patients enter their own reception area through a designated handicapped entrance, which complies with the Americans with Disabilities Act.

A special alcove in the main reception room is designed for new patient sign-in. Both reception rooms have small tables and chairs, which many people prefer over row chairs. The main reception room features machines that vend drinks, food, and a treat machine for children, who receive a free nickel to use in it after their appointment.

Following a new patient visit, the GD business staff mails a personalized letter of welcome plus our office brochure to the new patient's home. The brochure duplicates our two-page Yellow Pages ad on both sides of a single sheet of paper. USWest provides these four-color fliers for us. Our belief in the strength of the message in our ad is evidenced by its doubling as an office brochure. The ad says all we want to tell people about us. Sending the brochure to the patient's home allows other family members, relatives, neighbors, and friends the opportunity of learning our practice philosophy.

Each day our system prints out one of the most important documents we generate, for each of that day's appointed patients. This precious piece of paper is called a patient care form (PCF), which details fresh data about that patient, current to the moment (Fig. 4–13).

Information on the PCF includes address; telephone number and other personal numbers; medical alerts and timely notes; insurance coverage and special company requirements; other family information including last visits, last prophies, and last X-rays; and, finally, the patient's TP.

Prior to the visit, the PCF alerts staff to make proper preparations. At the outset of the visit—perhaps while an anesthetic becomes profound, or an impression sets—patients study the PCF, which is posted before them. In doing so, they update medical history and correct personal information. During the visit, the doctor works from the PCF as a guide to treatment.

Following the visit, notes are scribbled on it, before system entry. The business staff uses the PCF to check against the ledger, to assure billing data is properly entered. If surgery has been performed or a prosthesis seated, the PCF goes home with the doctor. Within 24 hours post-op and 48 hours post-seat, the patient will be called for a status report. No finer face can be painted upon internal marketing than is accomplished by a call from the dentist.

Each day, an armful of letters leaves GD, aimed at people who need to know how much we care, before they care how much we know. The letters are thank you for referral, welcome to the practice, thanks to other doctors for support or referral, collection and, yes, even referral to a new dentist. Nobody pleases everyone.

The letters are stock letters that are personalized with data like the patient's first name from the ledger. With a few keystrokes the letter can become the most personal letter the patient has ever received, well, since the last computerized letter he or she received. It has been said, and may be true, that the most beautiful sight in the world is a person's own name.

CHOOSING A NEW COMPUTER

There are three reasons to include some thoughts on choosing a new computer:

1. If you have never had a computer, someday you will.

2. If you now own a computer, you will trade up.

3. If you are happy with your current computer, you will upgrade it and add peripherals. When it comes to computers, change is the only thing that doesn't change.

In my book *Hands On: Dental Computers Made Easy,* I tell how to choose a new computer. No point in reinventing that wheel. However, several points are worth refreshing, even if you read *Hands On.*

For first-time users, computers are a bunch of switches that are easier to use than a typewriter and perform many tasks typewriters cannot. They do those jobs automatically, without having to hand-tool each task.

Do not, under any circumstances, fear a system that the average American eight-year-old has mastered. Despite your doubts, you are as smart as the eight-year-old. If you can turn on a light switch, open a combination padlock, and follow directions to make a box-mix cake, then you have all the skills needed to run a computer and not let it run you.

First-time users, don't believe the computer demonstration performed in your office. *Anything can be done on a demo.* Unless you see it work in an office as large as you want to become, it doesn't exist.

A demo system contains only a few charts that screen data at lightning speed. There is only one terminal, so you cannot watch several users access the system at the same time—a function your office team will require. There are no background jobs being done in a demo computer, which your team will demand. An in-office demo has deceptive potential.

First-time users, here are a couple of key points to remember. See the prospective computer system work in another dental office and learn from that office staff—not the computer salesperson—what features you absolutely must have. See several different systems before you judge. Do not buy price. Cheap is never better, even if every dental office in the nation has it.

Don't wait for computer technology to get finished, because it never will. Computerization is a journey, not a destination. While you drive your horse and buggy, people in automobiles will zoom past you on the dental highway to happiness.

Rid yourself of discount-house mentality. There's no such computer thing. The field is too ferociously competitive. Never buy dental software one place and the hardware another. That one piece of advice may be the best thing you've learned here.

Finally, dental management software buying decisions were never meant to be made by anyone other than a dentist. The smartest dental chairside assistant fully understands neither dental business needs nor the management tools the doctor wants. The best business assistant doesn't fully appreciate the clinical aspects of the system requirements, like the doctor does.

Forcing chairside assistants and receptionists to act in unfamiliar roles does you no credit, disserves your office, and abandons your professional responsibility. The dentist owns both the right brain and the left brain. Smart dentists use them both.

Computer people have told me that increasing numbers of dentists trade up to more powerful, functional, useful, and proven systems. They bought price and left brain, and assumed they would trade up later, when the staff got acquainted with computers or when the office learned some things computers could do for it, and when prices dropped.

Guess what? The staff learned to work computers in minutes. Staff learned to incorporate computer functions into the business of dentistry in days. Prices dropped, but new peripherals came out and the cycle was set to repeat.

Changing to a new system can be costly because the old system rarely has salvage value. Don't nickel and dime it. Just buy the best system available, if you are starting up, or scrap the old and start fresh with the best system you can find, if you are trading up.

There is only one other precaution: Don't wait. Your competitors aren't waiting. In the early 1960s, it didn't take our patients long to discover the difference between dentists who held high-speed handpieces and those who didn't. Our patients will detect the computer-dimension difference even faster. Why? Computer-oriented dentists will tell them.

THE EDO

When we understand right-brain functions a computer can perform, we are set to embark on a course of action leading to the EDO. The technical and mechanical things the GD office and personnel have done to reach this point are not relevant to this discussion. That's because we did it in a different time, and technology advances so rapidly, new methods outdate ours right along. The technical specifications of our system are listed later on.

Walk a new patient through my perception of an EDO to see what I have in mind. Understand that many electronic systems fuel this definition. To my knowledge, no single source peddles them all. This benefit allows dentists to acquire systems one at a time, without plunking down the family farm to get them all at once.

Anne, our new patient, approaches the front desk. She takes a seat in an alcove, where a health questionnaire is screened on a 17-inch, high-resolution, color monitor. The large color screen contains more dots than the usual monitor and therefore it screens pictures about four times more clearly than home televisions.

Anne responds to the questions by touching the screen to answer yes to a health history question, allergy, medical alert, or other important data. The receptionist types specific personal data in the new ledger she constructs.

The final screen of the health questionnaire tells Anne that she will be asked to sign a pad that electronically inputs her signature into the system. Anne's signature, she learns, admits four things:

1. she told the complete truth about her health history,

2. she agrees that her signature is for insurance purposes,

3. she allows the office to check her credit, and

4. she agrees that if there is ever a question about her billing or service, she will submit to binding arbitration.

Please note: The agreement to accept binding arbitration has not been tested in the Iowa courts. Most people sign away the right to sue in certain banking, stock brokerage, and insurance transactions.

However, do not adopt this aspect of our sign-in procedure without legal counsel.

Upon Anne's signing in, the receptionist alerts hygiene chairside assistants to her arrival. The notice appears on a dedicated monitor, which allows hygiene chairside assistants to become patient-time sensitive. A piece of equipment that performs only a single function is called "dedicated."

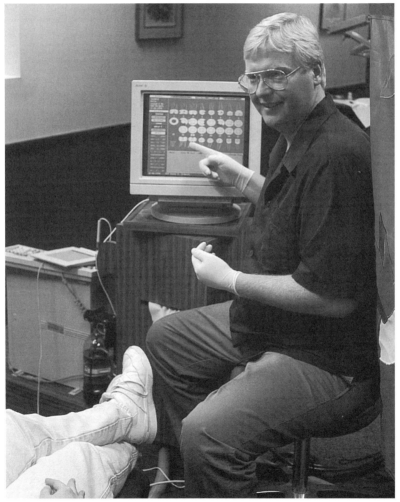

Fig. 4–14 Dr. James Knight explains tooth charting.

Fig. 4–15 Dr. Masih Safabakhsh demonstrates a CDR.

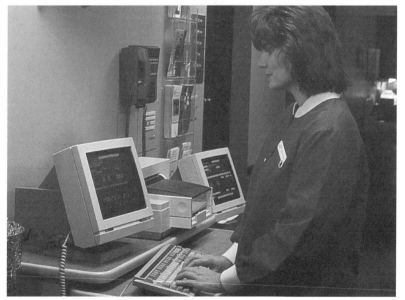

Fig. 4–16 Hygienist Catherine Schmidt creates a treatment plan.

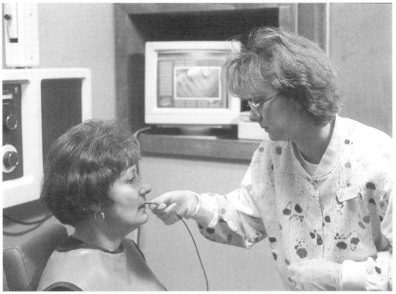

Fig. 4–17 Hygiene assistant Victoria Walker positions the CDR sensor.

Fig. 4–18 The denture area.

Fig. 4–19 An operatory chair.

Fig. 4–20
A treatment plan.

```
  28225-0        PATIENT TREATMENT PLAN        11/27/95
                    GENTLE DENTAL East, P.C.
```

For: Sue A. Doe
    123 Old Orchard Lane
    MARION   IA   52302

Service Description	Prv Tooth	Fee	Insurance	Patient
Treatment Phase				
Explanation	KNI			
Denture Data	KNI			
Payment Plans	KNI			
Subtotal		.00		.00
Treatment Phase 1				
1st Appt. +/- 60 min.	KNI			
RC Filling, 3 Canals	KNI UL 1st Molar			
Subtotal		.00		.00
Treatment Phase 2				
2nd Appt. +/- 60 min.	KNI			
Buildup, 1 Pin	KNI UL 1st Molar			
Crown Prep-1/2 Due	KNI UL 1st Molar			
Subtotal		.00		.00
Treatment Phase 3				
3rd Appt. +/- 30 min.	KNI			
Crown Porcelain	KNI UL 1st Molar			
Imp/Partial- 1/2 Due	KNI			
Subtotal		.00		.00
Treatment Phase 4				
4th Appt. +/- 15 min.	KNI			
Bite Block	KNI			
Subtotal		.00		.00
Treatment Phase 5				
5th Appt. +/- 30 min.	KNI			
Try In	KNI			
Subtotal		.00		.00
Treatment Phase 6				
6th Appt. +/- 30 min.	KNI			
Partial Lower Denture	KNI			
Subtotal		.00		.00
Treatment Phase 7				
7th Appt. +/- 30 min.	KNI			
Partial Adjustment	KNI			
Subtotal		.00		.00
Total:		.00		.00

Fig. 4–21 Treatment plan form.

GENTLE DENTAL   393-7000

DENTURE DATA: Gentle Dental will honor this denture plan for the next 3 months, after which it must be updated before it is performed. To maintain 1950s prices for 1990s dentures, we require 1/2 of the payment at the time impressions are taken and the balance paid BEFORE the denture is placed. Credit cards are accepted, however cash or check payments for seniors receive a 10% courtesy discount. THIS IS AN ESTIMATE ONLY.

EXPLANATION: Gentle Dental will honor this plan for the next 3 months. After that, it will need to be updated before it is begun. If this plan has been presented without first cleaning, X-raying, and examining the teeth, those procedures must be done before this plan can be perfected and performed. THIS IS AN ESTIMATE ONLY.

BUILD UP. Before putting a crown on a tooth, often we must replace missing parts of the tooth like old fillings or decay. Anchor pins are placed in the tooth and bonded plastics are used to rebuild the tooth.

BITE BLOCK: This increases the height of the lower face so that: 1. The jaw joint works better, and 2. The appearance becomes more nearly like 8-10 years ago. The trade-off is that chewing skills need to be relearned due to chewing at a new level.

CROWN PREP. To prepare for a crown we must remove the outer shell of enamel from the tooth, which is painlessly whisked away with high speed instruments. The sound, healthy part of the tooth is saved. It normally takes a week to make a crown.

1/2 of the crown fee is due at the time the crown prep is done.

CROWN. Crowns are precision-made thimbles of metal that fit over a tooth. They can be silver, gold, or covered with porcelain to look exactly like a tooth. Crowns restore the tooth for many years.

IMPRESSION: During this appointment, soft materials are placed in a tray and held next to mouth tissues until they have set firmly, like Jello sets up. These materials duplicate the mouth so that we can create as close a fit with your new denture as possible.

PARTIAL. A partial denture is an appliance you can take out and put back in as often as you wish. It is precision made to fill the spaces caused by lost teeth. Partials are plastic or metal, with metal being stronger, lighter, and usually fitting more snugly. Partials must be removed after each eating to clean food from

Fig. 4–22 Patient explanation.

beneath them. If proper cleaning isn't performed the teeth that hold the partials in may decay sooner than normal.

ROOT CANAL FILLING. Nerves die in teeth because of either an accident or decay. A dead tooth nerve festers like a splinter in your finger. So we must remove the nerve/splinter with tiny corkscrews that painlessly whisk away the bad parts. It's like taking a wick out of a candle. This leaves a hollow tube which we fill. 95% of all root canal fillings are successful.

TRY-IN: We set your denture teeth in wax and try them in, just to be sure we create a handsome and beautiful new look. Since we use wax to hold the teeth, we can easily make any adjustments needed. If you like, bring someone (whose opinion you value highly) with you to this appointment. You, the doctor, our staff, and your friend can then judge how nicely we created the "real you" look.

GENTLE DENTAL   393-7000

PAYMENT PLANS: Gentle Dental is pleased to offer a 10% courtesy discount for seniors when paying by check or cash for immediate payment in full, on the day of service. Additionally, we offer 5 methods of deferred payment: MasterCard Visa, Discover, American Express and our own, 12 month no-interest payment plan, administered for us by AVCO Finance. All deferred plans require credit worthiness, as determined by the finance resource.

COMMENTS :

Fig. 4–22 *(Continued)*

While Anne awaits the call to hygiene, the receptionist accesses a dedicated computer that employs software provided by the local outlet of a national credit bureau. She inputs Anne's name and social security number and, within seconds, a dedicated printer taps out a report of Anne's creditworthiness. In minutes, the receptionist has accessed more credit information about Anne than her family knows. A foundation now has been laid to help the office determine an acceptable financial plan for Anne. A PCF is created for Anne, to follow her to hygiene.

In moments a hygiene assistant calls for Anne and they go to X-ray, where a sensor is placed in Anne's mouth (Figs. 4–15, 4–17). In 1/100th of a second, a computerized dental radiograph (CDR) screens on a small monitor in the X-ray room. If the radiograph is incorrectly positioned, the assistant retakes it.

Anne is escorted to a hygiene chair where she meets the hygienist who then performs periodontal and tooth charting on separately screened charts, assisted by her chairside assistant (Fig. 4–14). Anne is positioned so that she can observe the process on the 17-inch color monitor, like the one in reception.

The initial prophylaxis is given and Anne is shown a video of standard flossing and brushing home care instructions. The doctor is brought to the chair to perform an examination, cancer screening, and diagnosis. Tooth and perio charts are reviewed on the screen, along with the X-rays which are called up for viewing by Anne with the dentist's guidance.

Anne's dental wishes are invited and her dental needs discussed with her. She learns that she will participate in the process of planning the best course for her future dental health. Following agreement on a plan, the chairside assistant assembles a treatment plan document (Fig. 4–16). The work is phased into appointments that list time estimates, and also show costs, insured and patient portions, an explanation of terms, and deferred payment options, for the patient portion (Figs. 4–20 through 4–22).

The chairside assistant reviews the data with Anne and invites her questions and input. Terms are explained, number and length of appointments discussed, financial requirements and options reviewed, and an initial appointment is made. The chairside assistant then escorts Anne to reception, where she pays today's estimated patient portion.

Her payment is made with a MasterCard, which is swiped through a recorder, with credit approval given instantly and a statement printed at once. Anne signs the statement, pockets her copy, and the office copy is recycled. Payment is put into the office bank account within 48 hours.

Anne leaves GD, carrying an appointment card, copies of her treatment plan, tooth and perio charts, and a home care brochure. Since Anne requires premedication, a prescription was printed for her, which listed data identifying her to the pharmacist and clearly (printed not scribbled) notes the dentist's drug of choice, plus listing precautions about this drug.

That evening, the system first creates, then batches her insurance statement and E-mails it to the insurance warehouse, where it is sent to arrive in the insurance company office the following morning.

The next day she receives a letter of welcome along with an office brochure. Her sister, who referred her to GD and who is also a GD patient, will receive a thank-you letter for the referral. Her former dentist will receive a letter requesting chart and X-rays. Prior to her next appointment, a list of appointed patients will be brought up on a screen, then called using software developed for the purpose.

When Anne returns for treatment, another PCF will be created. It will be used for preparing her tray, updating data and medical history, guiding the dentist's treatment, inputting treatment notes in her ledger, and will follow her to reception where charge and payment notes are confirmed. It will also go home with the doctor for a post-op/ post-treatment call.

She will view an informed consent video on the monitor before the chair and then sign her acceptance of the procedure, using a stylus on a mouse pad.

A lab tracker follows the preparation of a prosthesis for Anne, assuring that staff does not miss the seat date. In supply, a bar code program maintains a declining inventory on all supplies as they are taken from the supply room to enter the work areas. The supplier monitors this special computer on a modem, reordering supplies as needed.

When the computer calendar reaches trigger points (daily, weekly, monthly, quarterly, or annually), reports will generate and file in private files as needed for management review. Any report or document printed for Anne that is not either mailed or carried from the office is shredded and then saved for recycling. Biohazardous waste paper, of course, cannot be recycled. Because disposal costs are measured by volume, this material is first compressed in a compactor, then boxed and taken from the office by licensed collectors.

As our accountant requires office numbers, she pulls them from the system on a modem that goes directly into the general ledger systems of the office. Hard copy is not needed for this transfer of data.

Payroll is computed from a time clock that informs the employee how much time has been accumulated during a pay period. The value of this feature comes when the staff member nears the end of a time period and finds that she is close to going into overtime. GD does not permit overtime; therefore, the staff member is required to self-monitor the time, to not go into the time-and-a-half pay schedule overtime requires.

GD learned this need years ago, when an employee reported to the U.S. Department of Commerce that GD had failed to pay overtime. A review by the department resulted in our being required to pay several thousand dollars of back overtime. As the televison commercial says, "Certain restrictions apply."

Alert offices need to know all the rules that cover staff compliance in several departments of government (Fig. 4–23). Those that come quickly to mind are the IRS, OSHA, Fair Employment Practices Act, and the U.S. Department of Commerce. Rules that we once ignored because they only covered "real" businesses, suddenly apply to dentistry. Our profession has reached the vaunted status of being just as subject to fine as a manufacturer or retailer.

GIGO/WYSIWYG

Before we leave the neurology of this key nerve center called a computer, two computer acronyms seem to apply as well to us as to the device. GIGO stands for Garbage In Garbage Out. In other words, if billings and deposits are not correctly entered, for example, ending balances cannot be accurate.

Similarly, if in the process of choosing the main system or aspects of a system to employ, we input mental garbage, there is less chance for good choices to result. How do we know it's garbage? How did you choose your handpiece, your office space, or your home? You studied, you compared, you assessed the market, you did your homework. Nothing important is ever easy. Your computer choice will influence your dental future more than any other decision you will ever make. Let no one make it for you, not staff, not computer sales personnel, not me. It's your choice. Make it wisely.

WYSIWYG is another useful acronym. (It is pronounced exactly the way it looks—wis, as in whistle, long e, wig.) WYSIWYG means What

You See Is What You Get. In a computer it means hard copy will print with a layout that looks the same as the screened appearance. Applied to the human mind, the acronym works equally well.

What we see in our mind will be what we will get. As we point to the EDO—and that is where we are all headed—dentists with a clear vision of where they are going will get there. Those who can't see it, won't.

JOHN VINCENT ATANASOFF, INVENTOR

Nine-year-old John Vincent Atanasoff did something most nine-year-olds don't. He figured out how to use his father's slide rule.

Then he quickly went through his mother's college algebra book. When he graduated from the University of Florida with a nearly perfect grade point average in electrical engineering, he accepted a teaching position at Iowa State University (ISU) in Ames.

While at ISU, he earned a master's degree in mathematics and taught, and thought. A great many of his thoughts dealt with how to compute a series of problems more rapidly than by hand. For months he struggled to find a way to solve the problem of speeding up mathematical solutions.

Late on a cold winter afternoon in 1938, John V. Atanasoff got in his car and started driving, an exercise he found cleared his mind. As he drove he mused on his mathematical problems, feeling that a solution was nearby, just eluding his mental grasp.

He drove east of Ames on Highway 30, then south to Highway 6, through small Iowa towns until he reached the Mississippi River, and across into Illinois. By now it was dark and the lights of a tavern beckoned. He went in, hung up his heavy coat, and ordered a drink, lost in his thoughts.

An hour or two went by and gradually the haze that covered his problem parted and the young professor saw, for the first time, the elements he needed. He decided to:

1. use electronics for speed,

2. defy the decimal (base-ten)   system and use the binary (base-two) system,

3. use condensers for memory and use regenerative or "jogging" process to avoid lapses caused by a leakage of power, and

4. compute by direct logical action, and not by enumeration as in analog calculating devices.

Atanasoff requested funds to hire an assistant and build a prototype of his computer. The school gave him a small grant which he used to hire Iowan Clifford Berry, a brilliant young graduate student. Over the next months the two mathematical geniuses labored together, each synergistically complementing the other's thoughts, creating a crude device that worked well enough to prove them right. Atanasoff named their device the Atanasoff Berry Computer.

As World War II began, both Atanasoff and Berry were called into the military support services. Neither had the time nor was in a position to assure that patent applications were properly pursued. To their everlasting regret, the college failed to apply for patents that would have eventually yielded billions of dollars in royalties both to ISU and to the inventors.

There was another problem. A fellow scientist, John Mauchly, a physicist at Ursinus College, just north of Philadelphia, had been a guest in Atanasoff's home, and Atanasoff had naively revealed to him detailed drawings, plans, theories, and the working model of his first computer.

Mauchly quietly prepared his own version of the computer, then fashioned a deal with the U.S. Army to build the Electronic Numerical Integrator and Computer (ENIAC) for use in computing ballistics trajectories. Since the ENIAC was considered top secret, Atanasoff could not gain access to either the device or the patents for which Mauchly was quick to file.

Years later, when Mauchly had become known as the father of the computer due to ENIAC, other large computer companies contested the patents that Mauchly sold to the Sperry Rand Corporation. Their motive was purely economic, as Sperry Rand planned to charge exorbitant fees for their use.

The trial was one of the longest and costliest in history, with more than $5 million spent by Sperry Rand and $3 million by the Honeywell Company, not counting court costs, for a seven-year trial that stretched to more than 20,000 pages of trial transcripts.

When the trial ended, Judge Earl Larson unequivocally found that Mauchly's ENIAC was "derived from Atanasoff and that the invention claimed in the Mauchly patent was derived from Atanasoff." Larson ruled that Mauchly's computer patent was invalid and Atanasoff clearly emerged the winner.

Iowan Dr. John Vincent Atanasoff simply reinvented civilization. Dentistry will one day follow suit.

THE GD COMPUTER SYSTEM

The Gentle Dental computer system consists of the following, plus the credit card connection, supply system, and credit bureau connection, as stated in the text.

A 486-66 MHz server-unit, running SCO XENIX with 32 megabytes of random access memory and a 1 gigabyte SCSI hard disc. The server offers Ethernet connectivity to a 16-port hub, as well as RS-232 "intelligent" serial connectivity for up to 32 workstations or printers. We have three 14,400-baud modems for dial-in and dial-out services connected to our server, enabling us to work from home and on the road . . . and to support dial-out services like our Electronic Insurance Claims Processing.

We have 10 workstations we refer to as "smart stations." They also are high-speed 486 units with 16 MB of random access memory, 540 MB hard disc drives with Ethernet, serial, and parallel connectivity. The workstations currently run MS-DOS, Windows, and UNIX programs simultaneously. They also have integrated television and video, support our TWAIN compliant scanner, SCSI Floptical Disks, and are operated by keyboard, tablets, or mice.

We have dot-matrix, laser, ink-jet, and color ink-jet printers from CANON, Hewlett Packard, and OKIDATA. Approximately 15 more ASCII "dumb" stations connect to our server, supporting two pages of memory connected through RS-232.

We also have a lot of wire.

DISSECTION LAB

The goal is to improve the quality of the dental experience through the intelligent use of smart machines. The right-brain, left-brain theory gives us a metaphor for application of dental computers. The left brain counts the beans. The right brain produces beans to count.

Left-brain functions include billing, accounts receivable, payroll, electronic insurance claims processing, general ledger, payables, and job schedules, plus management records generated from those documents. These functions are systems driven.

Right-brain functions are the clinical aspects of dentistry, and include clinical notes, word processing, scheduling, referral, treatment planning, and internal marketing. These aspects of our computer make the practice patient sensitive.

External marketing was shown to be Yellow Pages, Time & Temperature, and newspaper advertising, and we talked about how people choose a dentist. Internal marketing discussion focused on office decor, the PCF, and office letters.

A dentist cannot delegate choosing a new computer. This key job is not a staff duty. A patient was taken through the EDO to illustrate how we at GD perceive an EDO to be. Electronic peripherals of informed consent video, lab tracker, time clock, inventory and supply control, and external accounting were noted.

It is deemed important, to assure office compliance with the myriad of employment laws, to post the standard "required posting for employees." This document alerts staff to their rights.

Required Postings

Employers are required by state and federal laws to display certain posters prominently in the workplace. The general requirements and ordering points are listed below.

State Government

• Job Insurance (Available in English and Spanish)	Required of all employers covered by the Law.	Department of Employment Services 1000 East Grand Avenue Des Moines, IA 50319 515-281-4426; 1-800-562-4692 (V/TDD)
• OSHA Injuries and Illnesses Log and Summary (must be posted annually during February)	Required of employers in high rate industries having more than 10 workers.	Department of Employment Services Labor Services Division 1000 East Grand Avenue Des Moines, IA 50319 515-281-3606; 1-800-562-4692 (V/TDD)
• Safety & Health Protection on the Job	Required of all employers.	Labor Services Division (See above)
• Your Rights Under Iowa's Minimum Wage	Required of all employers covered by the Law.	Labor Services Division (See above)
• Equal Employment Opportunity is the Law	Recommended.	Iowa Civil Rights Commission 211 East Maple Street, 2nd Flr. Des Moines, IA 50319 515-281-4121 1-800-457-4416 (within Iowa)

Federal Government

• Employee Polygraph Protection Act	Required of all employers covered by the Law.	Employment Standards Administration Wage and Hour Division 643 Federal Building 210 Walnut Street Des Moines, IA 50309 515-284-4625
• Family & Medical Leave Act	Required of all employers covered by the Law.	Wage and Hour Division (See above)
• Notice to Employees— Federal Minimum Wage	Required of all employers covered by the Law.	Wage and Hour Division (See above)
• Equal Employment Opportunity is the Law (Available in English and Spanish)	Required of all employers.	EEOC Publications Center P.O. Box 12549 Cincinnati, Ohio 45212 1-800-669-3362

Department of Employment Services

An Equal Employment Opportunity Agency

70-8030 (9-93)

Fig. 4–23 Required posting for employees.

===========◈===========

CHAPTER FIVE

RESPIRATORY— A BREATH OF FRESH AIR

In the next few paragraphs you will learn three words that will deliver all the new patients you can handle. The only stipulations are, you must first want them, and you must be able to care for them.

That may sound like a dichotomy. It isn't. If a half-dozen new welfare patients waited for you to open your office doors tomorrow morning, *would* you treat them? If six new fee-for-service patients waited for you to open your doors tomorrow morning, *could* you care for them? Don't feel remiss. Few offices either would or could solve either of those dilemmas.

A dentist friend questioned me about his pending new office. I helped only because he's a friend. (Office consultation is *not* my thing.) He wondered if he should open an office in a new shopping center, and then he wondered if he could get the new business he would need to sustain growth. The more I think of what I told him, the more it seems appropriate for these pages.

I asked him when I could get an appointment as a new patient in his current office. His wife, who quadruples as the mother of their four children, homemaker, office manager, and receptionist, said she could book me in about seven weeks. My friend, I told him, you've got a serious problem, a surfeit of goodness.

Our office attracts a new patient every hour we are open. We open at 7 A.M. and close at 8 P.M. We gear for that program, having spent years developing the technique, the staff, the facilities, and the mindset to allow it to happen. But my colleague is strangled by today, unable to embrace a tomorrow of growth.

We all—and I include myself and my office—build barriers that prevent us from achieving all that we might. Some hurdles are constructive. Some are destructive. However, to understand how to cause dental practice growth, it takes only three words: Remove the barriers!

Filling dental chairs is no more complicated than that. What obstacles prevent us from growth? All the ones we have erected. Do we speak Spanish? If not, we restrain Spanish-speaking people from our practice. Are we open at 6 A.M.? Then we restrict people who want early A.M. appointments.

Does our office phone ring a half-dozen times before it is answered? Barrier. Do we have a harried or curt-sounding receptionist? Barrier. Are our fees posh? Barrier. Can someone in urgent need get a dental appointment to see us today? Barrier. Will a human being answer our office phone at 2 A.M.? Barrier. Will we refer out endodontic needs? Barrier.

Do we not have free parking? Barrier. Is our office not located near well-traveled traffic routes? Barrier. Do we not have nitrous oxide available for our patients? Barrier. Do we fail to tell about ourselves in the Yellow Pages? Barrier. Do we fail to offer deferred payment plans? Barrier. Did we fail to become an EDO? Barrier.

The point is, we each erect our own fences, keeping away those we want kept out. Few dentists view practice growth quite that way. Colleagues who seek new patients have a hard time believing that practice growth follows when they simply reduce the ways they keep people out of their practices!

Of course, we all have barriers we refuse to remove. I refuse to study Chinese. Don't look for me at the chair on Saturday. I wouldn't dream of working for substandard fees. Implants? Me? Never. Work until 8 P.M.? No way, my friend. I won't finance deferred payment plans to our office. Orthodontics doesn't trip my trigger.

All those barriers are mine. I built them so I must live with them. How can my practice overcome my barriers? That's easy. Hire people who lower the barriers I have raised. To that end, I hire associates who will work Saturdays and evenings. Barriers dropped.

We seek staff with foreign language ability and a fence gets taken down. We look for doctors who will introduce new dimensions into the practice, such as implants, grafts, dentures, second molar endodontics, and bony impaction extractions. When we succeed, blockades tumble. We offer a wide spectrum of deferred payment options. Obstruction over. We position our fees to be competitive. Barrier dropped. Next question.

Instead of wondering what you can do to attract new patients, think instead of all the hurdles you have created to keep new patients out of your practice. My friend, who couldn't see me as a new patient for almost two months, has erected a giant barrier that insulates him from growth. He needs an associate, as quickly as possible.

With an associate he can lower his barriers of hours, accept more welfare, gain new skills and professional perspectives in his office, and maybe allow his fees to settle into a more competitive range. Whatever features he may add, when he hires an associate, he will lower barriers he now cannot. Dental practice growth is not much more complicated than that.

There is no question we must render a good dental experience. Fail that and we build a mountainous obstacle to success. Failing to disclose full financial information to our patients fences away people who need to know.

To obtain new business, we must express our availability through information devices called advertising—which means, to announce. Hide our talents under a bushel basket and our light will never shine the way it should.

If we want new business, we employ capable staff, position our practice in a good location, create and access the right traffic patterns, fill the office with enough chairs, embrace productive attitudes, and utilize systems that work. When we fail those proven steps, we keep away people whose lives would be enriched by being served with our skills. The upshot is: To get new business, we don't need to drag bodies in, just stop keeping them out!

THE TREATMENT PLAN

Some pages ago, the value of those priceless TP pages was noted. Think of them now in this new light. When an office does not provide printed treatment plans to its patients, those patients will talk to patients who are treated by dentists who do. They will justifiably wonder why they got shorted.

Patients who have not received the benefits of full disclosure will judge their dentist to be unwilling to fulfill patient information needs. Fair or not, that judgment keeps new patients at bay.

Dentists who refuse to lower their barriers are not wrong. The American system avails each of us the right to fail any way we want to. However, if we don't achieve the success we feel is our due, know that our own barriers prevent us, and we can fault no one else.

It seems natural to resent forced change. Having lived through four-and-a-half decades of dentistry, I admit there were times when I felt some of that same anger. For a couple of years after high-speed handpieces came on the scene, I refused to buy one. I even concocted a cute little excuse that went, "A lot of slow-speed dentists are going to get into a lot of trouble with high-speed handpieces." All pure sour grapes, of course.

So, if you feel a bit put out at being forced into computer progress, I surely understand and completely sympathize. The trouble is, computers are cooking new recipes for success in dental offices all over town these days. Competition is hot, and getting hotter, with the magnitude of computer benefits fueling the fire. We may not like the heat, but if we are going to stay in the kitchen, we must deal with it.

Whatever values are attached to treatment planning go double for financial planning. There isn't a whole lot more I want to say about finances except to suggest avoiding listening to anyone discuss collection letters. That's because collection problems occur before a tooth is ever touched.

When we properly present a treatment plan and offer deferred payment options, check credit, and require office credit approval prior to commencing treatment—collection problems become mostly history (Fig. 5–1). In the next chapter I'll deal with management measures, but having

Fig. 5–1

said what I just said about collections being our fault, I will add that GD does accumulate some uncollectible accounts.

What do we do with them? Often small balances are more nuisance than they are worth. Our debtors often have imagined grievances with us, and we may end up with a lawsuit or with a small claims court to cope with. Years ago we developed a technique for settling the small balance account.

The approach has worked reasonably well, and allows us to write these balances off the books, rather than continually throwing good money—through repeated statements—after bad. When the account reaches the 120-day column in our aging of accounts receivable, we send this letter:

> Dear Joe:
>
> My accountant tells me you have a balance due this office of $22.00. Perhaps you have overlooked the

matter or maybe there's another reason. Is it one of the following?

___ I am unemployed (or on strike).

___ I intend to honor this debt and do not want it on my credit history.

___ I am unhappy with Gentle Dental services because:_____

_____

_____

If you feel we were unfair in our fees, please reduce them to what you think is fair, and pay that amount. We will then consider the debt paid in full. We want to be fair but, at the same time, we have costs that must be met, too. We value you as an important person and do not want this debt to cloud our friendship.

Sincerely,

Duane A. Schmidt, D.D.S.

SELLING DENTISTRY

I'm not sure I know how to sell dentistry, much less tell you how to do it. Whatever I know has been the hard-knocks school of learning it the tough way. When I learned to say less, and say it in English, I sold more space maintainers. I've learned to ask questions and let my patients talk more. Generally, if I can put my ego on hold, they usually will sell themselves on the right course of action.

When I was a pedodontist, an orthodontist some years my senior was my mentor. He told me that if I never hard-sold anyone I would sleep soundly every night. He was right. When I was in college, I luckily was hired to sell ladies' shoes. On my first day, the boss taught me to never show a woman three pairs of shoes at one time. "She won't buy any, if you do that," he warned.

He taught me first to show my customer two pairs of shoes. If the lady wanted to see another pair, I was to ask her which of the shoes before her she liked best. When she pointed to one pair, I took the other pair away and replaced them with the pair she wanted to see. Now, she faced only a choice between two pairs, not three. After I learned that pattern, I sold a lot of shoes. I'm sure the psychology works for men the same way.

Guess how many kinds of dentures we sell today at Gentle Dental? Guess how many kinds of crowns we sell? Guess how many kinds of treatment plans we generally try to develop? If you guessed two, you hit it right on the head. Two is an easy number for both staff and patients to cope with. More than two choices is, well, a barrier. The method seems to work for us.

If any reader has a gender hangup, and believes that I do, you may be right, but not the way you think. In the 1980s, I wrote an article that *Dental Economics* published titled, "The Hand that Rocks the Cradle Rules the Dental World." The numbers have surely changed, but anyone who doesn't believe that women control the world of business is not paying attention.

Women make more buying decisions than men in virtually any category: Travel, automobiles, homes, dining out, liquor, wine, secondary education, clothing, cosmetics, and jewelry. The list is endless. Women control most of the world's wealth, real estate, and stocks. More new companies on the stock exchange are owned or controlled by women.

Walk into Bloomingdale's in New York City, Marshall Field in Chicago, and Macy's in San Francisco. Tell me the first thing you see when you enter these, and all other, fine department stores.

Here's what we see: Cosmetics, handbags, lingerie, costume jewelry, and women's gloves and accessories. Facetiously I ask, let's guess whether these shrewd retailers all accidentally placed their most popular female sales attractions just inside the ground-floor doors? Where is the men's department? Maybe, third floor, in the rear.

Smart retailers have recognized this female bias for years. Check the decor in malls, fine restaurants, hotels, resorts, theaters, and other fine extablishments which men and women both patronize. There is undeniable partiality in pleasing the female taste, and we dentists will do well to exercise resourceful prejudice in pleasing the female palate.

One special statistic from that article sticks in my mind: Women make 84 percent of all dental appointments. I do indeed have a female bias in my perception of marketing, and it is founded on this belief: Women control the purchase of most dental services.

To create our new look in the fashionable Gentle Dental office, I consulted with people who understood how to create environs with feminine appeal. The compliments we receive and the growth of our business both confirm that my advisors—many of whom were ladies on staff—hit the fingernail right on the head.

NLP

Nearly a decade ago, a dental colleague praised a technique she used with great success to enhance the dental experience. A lady dentist friend told me it was called neuro-lingual programming (NLP), a technique of subliminal persuasion that apparently employs some low-level hypnotic techniques. I'm not sure of that definition, so cut me some slack, please.

I cannot give a scholarly dissertation on something I know so little about. Despite my lack of academic insight, you may find a story here with merit. The lesson I learned from the experience I had with NLP has stood me in good stead.

Go with me to the Hotel Fontainebleau in Miami. The year: 1987. It's a Thursday evening in January and I've just finished a fine dinner. As I enjoy an after-dinner glass of wine and cup of coffee, I light a cigarette and relish the moment.

Tomorrow, I will deliver a half-day talk to a convention. It's going to be fun. These are sharp people, a group of keen minds, and we always enjoy a lot of give and take. I've been with this group before, so we know each other.

My dinner companion is a book, the one I read on the flight to Miami. The book is titled *Turtles All the Way Down* (Judith DeLozier and John Grinder). It's a fascinating read that introduces NLP, but I'm not sure I fully understand the technique. My friend put me onto this book and several others, which I devoured in pursuit of learning more about the NLP program she had endorsed.

I finished the book, lit another cigarette, and reflected on what I had just read. If I understood it correctly, my conscious mind could communicate with another person's subconscious mind to help alter that person's behavior. I recall that one of the examples was how to help someone lose weight.

The thought occurred, if my conscious mind can talk to another person's subconscious mind, why can't I talk to my own subconscious? I thought I'd test the idea, but in order to change something in one's own life there must be something the person wants changed.

There's the rub. What in the world would I want to change? Several minutes went by as I tried to think of some one thing in my life that I might want changed. Then I saw it. The cigarette in my fingers. I had smoked nearly 80 cigarettes that day, and every day, for years.

My problem was, I didn't want to quit. I liked to smoke. I was psychologically and physically addicted. My daughters had gifted me with a beautiful gold Dunhill lighter and cigarette case, the fancy stuff. I liked the ritual and the nicotine rush that my body demanded.

Then it dawned on me. The best test of the NLP program would be to see if I could change behavior that I did not want changed. Sure, I knew all the smoking statistics. I reeked with that knowledge as well as of smoke. Between each patient, I smoked a full cigarette, almost always one while waiting for an anesthetic to become profound, and for an impression to gel and cement to set. No one hassled me to quit, and it was not even remotely my priority.

This has got to be one whale of a test of NLP, I thought, and so I went through the little litany that I perceived was the technique. I'm not sure it was the correct NLP routine to this day, but bear with me. Here's the entire speech, exactly as I recall giving it to myself.

"Okay, subconscious mind, we both know that smoking is not smart. I want you to find a substitute for smoking that will work in my body and simply install it. You don't need to tell me what you choose as a replacement. However, before you install something, check it against my other systems to make sure I won't be worse off than before." That was it. I had another cigarette and went to bed.

If you've never been an addict, you may not know the lengths we go to appease that little guy that controls our life. We wake up in the middle of the night for a cigarette. We stop a meal to have a smoke. We slip out during a Sunday sermon to grab a quick puff. In those days smokers were not segregated and could foul the air everywhere, which was exactly where I smoked.

We smoking addicts fail to do another filling for our patient, because we need a fix. We stop short some of life's most pleasurable moments, to suck a cigarette. Now, that's a true addict. In the morning, everyone else goes to the bathroom the minute their feet hit the floor. Not us smokers. We light up first.

The next morning, I was in the middle of breakfast when I suddenly realized I had not had my quota of three to four cigarettes by that time. In panic I slapped my jacket pocket, to see if I had my cigarette case with me. I did. Lighter there, too. Whew! I'll have a smoke when I finish breakfast, I decided.

I was in the meeting room, checking the sound, lighting, and seating when I realized I once again had forgotten to smoke. People started to filter in and smoking on platform is out. I'll smoke at break, I thought.

When the meeting began, I walked around in front of the speaker's stand, scrapped my notes, and told the group, "I don't know what's happening in my life today, but something different is surely going on." Then I delivered probably my best talk, ever.

At break time, my friends gathered around to visit and ask questions, and I could not get away to smoke. When I finished, one of the doctors asked if I'd like to go sailing. In January, you don't ask a frozen Iowan that question twice. Of course I would, and did. I got through the day without a single cigarette. Every day since, too.

The way I used this probably poor imitation of the NLP technique has stood me in good stead time after time. When I want something, I simply program it in my mind. It seems like events follow my programs. Maybe it happens because there's truth in something called "self-fulfilling prophecy."

Anyway, that's my story. Yes, I've used what I conceive to be NLP with my patients. Pedodontists know that a steady stream of soft talk placates a youngster. Maybe that's something like NLP. Maybe it isn't. Whatever works, works. Right?

An added note: At GD we now counsel people who want to stop smoking. If a patient wants it, we prescribe the nicotine patch, all without charge, of course. It feels good to help others free their lives from addiction.

THE FIRST CAST GOLD CROWN

In the 1890s a gold crown to restore a broken-down tooth cost only $5. There were two problems with that: It took hours and hours to earn $5, and the crowns—swedged, by beating soft gold into shape on a die—wore out in months.

In Iowa, Denison dentist B.F. Philbrook was concerned about the short life of those $5 crowns. He hunted for a way to make a less costly crown that would last. When he learned how jewelry was cast out of an alloy of gold, which was far stronger than the 24K gold, he reasoned that a tooth crown could also be cast.

Dr. Philbrook reported his success in a turn-of-the-century article in the *Iowa Dental Journal*. His report gathered dust for more than a decade until other dentists discovered his finding and copied his process and results.

One dentist tried to patent Dr. Philbrook's process and began charging royalties on every cast crown dentists made. The ADA became involved in a lawsuit to break the gold crown patent and won when a researcher discovered Dr. Philbrook's *Iowa Dental Journal* article.

We don't need to be reminded how the cast restoration has truly changed the face of dentistry.

DISSECTION LAB

In this section, we took note that dentists raise barriers that keep people out of our offices. When we lower those fences, we allow people to flood into our practices. If we cannot lower them enough in a solo practice, we should consider acquiring associates to help open our offices to the people we force out. We don't need to drag bodies in. We just need to stop keeping them out.

Treatment plans herald the new age of communication dentistry that will occur because people will demand them, once they know that they are available options. They will become a standard of care that, in their absence, will mark the practice as below par.

Collection problems were noted to be creatures caused by improper financial arrangements, credit checking, and treatment planning. A simple collection letter for small balances was shown.

I confessed to not having all the answers about selling dentistry, but did note several rules I have followed successfully:

1. don't hard-sell,

2. don't oversell, and

3. offer only two alternatives, if you want a choice to be made.

The influence women have on the economy and particularly on dental economy was defined.

A form of the NLP programming was shown to be effective in programming wished-for results.

CHAPTER SIX

———◆———

DIGESTIVE APPARATUS

"He acquired a fortune,
and then a fortune acquired him."
—BION, 280 B.C.

When we have some month left over at the end of our money, it can get pretty scary out, can't it? You probably have had those months, just like I have. In the 1950s, my daughter Cyd was born in the welfare ward of a state teaching hospital.

I recall giving the doctor a $5 pair of cuff links, for bringing us such a beautiful baby. It was about all the cash we had. He knew it, and as he stood there on his front porch, tears streamed down his cheeks. I like a man that strong. No, those weren't the good old days. They were hard times.

Opening Gentle Dental in the mid-1970s, I tried to borrow $16,000 to buy some used equipment and give me operating capital for a couple of months. I had just come from my six-digit loss lesson that taught me to stay in a field I knew and to keep my business ego under wraps.

The bank turned me down. "Duane, there's already too many dentists in town," my banker cautioned.

That answer devastated my plans, until I remembered something called a sale-leaseback. Taking some furniture and a typewriter from home to my office, I sold them to a leasing company, then leased the items back. That raised the capital I needed, and I was off to prove the town needed one more dentist.

Those comments about my plunges into penury preface this chapter's discussion of the measures of a practice, a workable financial philosophy, and goals that can be met (Fig. 6–1). Because I've been beat in financial games and been broke and pretty well busted, my viewpoint about money reflects my banging into the walls going down the financial hallway of life.

Many money men and women differ on how to get cash and what to do with it once you find some. We each must decide which course we want to follow, but we cannot evaluate the differences until we know what they are. I can only speak for one view, mine. You are the judge.

My friend, John Wilde, practices in Keokuk, Iowa, and holds forth on some excellent ideas about gaining wealth and garnering security. I would suggest that his concepts should be required reading for dentists. You've probably read his articles in *Dental Economics* and perhaps his best-seller, *Bringing Your Practice Into Focus* (PennWell Books, 1993).

Good friends that we are, we don't completely see eye-to-eye on investments. He's tough to argue with, for, starting at zero, John has in his forty-some years of life acquired a trove of treasure. He and I differ in that I think he wants to accumulate golden eggs, and I want to own the goose that lays them.

MEASURES OF A PRACTICE

Since the course that I've charted through dentistry has been at times rocky, it certainly hasn't been the path many would choose. You don't climb mountains by staying in the valleys, and I'm not a valley person. A few years ago, I climbed Grand Teton to the 11,000-foot level.

MANAGEMENT MEASURES

1. **New Patient Flow**
2. **Accounts Receivable**
3. **Productivity**

Fig. 6–1 Management measures.

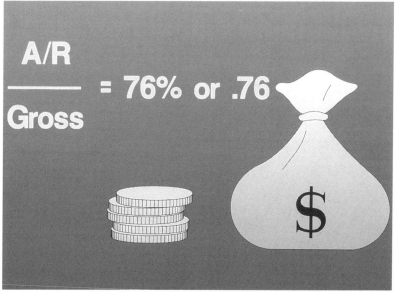

Fig. 6–2 A/R over gross.

This huge sentinel shadows the western sun that aims its twilight at Jackson, Wyoming.

When we plopped down on the flat rocks where we would bed that night, we were whipped but exhilarated. We sat on ledges with our feet dangling over dropoffs of thousands of feet. Night hunkered down over the mountain, and we listened to the grunts and groans of glaciers creaking down the draws, and heard crashing boulders race back to the bottom of the mountain where they once must have been an eon ago.

As we watched, entranced and breathless in the crisp air, one of our foursome reminded the rest of us, "Feast your eyes, guys. Very few people ever get to see this view."

Silently, we each nodded and seared the sights and sounds into our memory. We knew that to reach this height required an investment in time, money, stamina, and more than anything, the will to be there. Those barriers kept this awesome aerie pristine and precious and made its value priceless.

The four billion people living and breathing below us had their own mountains to climb, their own choices to pursue, their own investments of time, money, stamina, and will to make. None of us were right or wrong. We were all only different.

I did not set out to build a huge Gentle Dental. If I had thought GD might become what it has, I probably would have been scared off. The same thing happens in raising kids. Before our children are born, we fearfully ask, how do parents handle teens? Then that testy time comes and goes, and parents learn that while their children grew up, so did they. The same thing happens with building a dental practice.

Colleagues have told me they don't want to have a huge practice because of the management time it takes. As you have seen, through this book, once patterns are set, policies defined, and people trained to fulfill roles of responsibility, the time it takes to manage GD is probably less than the time required to manage a three-person office.

I cannot really think of one detail of practice, one management function, one measure of results that is different from your office to mine. Let's look at measuring success and see what I mean. The numbers I watch are few and simple. The computer system generates them on cue.

WEEKLY

Each week a printout of production by provider, number of appointments, and total number of new patients is generated and stored in a file. The file is accessed and I look to see if we are attracting a steady flow of new patients and if the business is about where I expect it to be.

Since I am a right-brained person, numbers are difficult for me, so I keep them very simple. I divide weekly production by two, and add two zeroes to estimate annual production. I do the same with the number of new patients—divide by two and add a couple of zeroes to get an annual number. (This is the same as multiplying by 50 weeks.)

MONTHLY

I look at four numbers only:

1. Production, which I multiply by 12 to annualize,

2. New patients, which I also multiply by 12 to annualize,

3. Front-desk collections to see if they meet the goal of 40 percent cash collections, and

4. Accounts receivable over production to measure against the goal of 76 percent.

Those numbers are all I check, and you can see it takes seconds. I learn a lot by taking a pulse and blood pressure on a patient. These numbers act as pulse and blood pressure for the practice.

The accounts receivable over production number speaks to staff performance in performing financial arrangements (Fig. 6–2). If they don't get done, we strengthen the emphasis during individual and staff meetings and tighten our watch on treatment starts. Sometimes the problem comes from doctors too eager to perform before they have gone through the required steps. The problem might be the front desk, allowing credit terms that conflict with office policy.

The dental industry, I am told, seeks 150 percent as the proper goal. That would mean, for example, in a practice with $50,000 of monthly production, accounts receivable could be $75,000 and be acceptable. In our practice, using those same numbers, we would require accounts receivable of $38,000 to meet our goal of 76 percent of production. The difference means that $37,000 of your money sits in someone else's pocket—not the place where it should be.

Just as patients sometimes have more serious tests performed, once in a while we may dig deeper into the numbers. For example, annually we may measure referral sources. This number should be a 2 to 1 ratio of new patients from family and friends over new patients from external advertising.

Infrequently, we may perform an analysis of accounts receivable, assuring that most of it is from insurers. We may then look into ledgers to determine what we forgot to do that caused any debt to age.

I fail to understand what is so complicated about dental management numbers. There are so few that mean anything important. When I watch computer system demos, I see reams of important-sounding-looking-feeling documents that those systems generate to supposedly manage the socks off a dental practice. Overmanaged, I'd say.

When our numbers indicate faults, good management means we diagnose the trouble and cure the illness. For example, if my front-desk collections drop, the problem could be that assistants are failing to make proper financial arrangements at the chair and/or (it could be some of both) receptionists are not collecting at the exit point.

Fortunately, everyone who enters the computer system leaves tracks that easily can be followed. In this way, we learn who on staff needs help and can fashion methods to bring his or her skills in line with others. Those methods may include reminding, reteaching, or even replacing. Too many people depend on this business to put the good of one person ahead of the good of all.

GOALS

Other than the two production goals, the one when staff won a trip to Mexico and the quest they are now on, we don't set goals. I don't like goal setting—never have, never will. A goal is a limit, it clearly states you do not expect to exceed it, thus top-siding opportunity. There are no limits so why should I place some on myself or on my staff?

Many dental computer systems have the ability to punch in daily production goals. In my biased view, daily production goals warp a practice in directions it has no business going. There is but one meaningful goal, and it is to provide quality dentistry within the format of a quality dental experience. When good dentistry and good experiences walk out the door, more business will walk in that same door than we can handle.

A goal puts the emphasis on the doctor and staff, removing the focus of our effort, which must always remain on the patient. For years I have not worn expensive jewelry or had money in my pocket when I go to the chair. I do not want my judgment sidetracked by my monetary interest in the outcome of this patient encounter. When the doctor's interests overshadow the patient's, the whole practice isn't worth a hill of spit.

As I said, I didn't set out to build a Gentle Dental giant. Over the years, my gray hair and some gray matter taught me that the focus must remain, solely, wholly, and only on what is best for my patient. I have not always succeeded, but I have never failed to maintain that vision.

I did not set out to build a huge practice. I merely set out to pinpoint the barriers to my practice success I had erected, and then concoct ways to remove them. Once they started to fall away, the business was there.

There is another element. My right-brain inclinations give me an advantage in resolving problems and give me a willingness to gamble. A dentist entrepreneur willingly rolls the dental dice. Some people are suited for that and some not.

In the beginning of my current practice, I decided to build something that would retire me and survive me. Many dentists build a practice, then plan to sell it off and walk away. That's not wrong. Sometimes, however, they leave it before their plan is fulfilled. Then the practice becomes a distress sale and the only residue comes from prudent investing, during the dentist's lifetime.

In secure investment programs that employ fixed-return instruments, single-digit annual earnings are currently common and about the best that can be expected. Those golden eggs grow steadily in the nest, but never rapidly.

At the same time, returns from a viable practice should easily reach double- or triple-digit levels. That level of return holds more of my interest. As I see it, a surviving practice is the goose that lays those golden eggs.

A number of steps had to be taken to reach a stage of survivability. Renaming the office to Gentle Dental from "Dr. Schmidt's Dental Office" was an early step. Bringing associates into the practice was another. My plan continued by setting up programs to create a solid business plan, aimed at a steady market niche.

Hiring and training management people, and giving them management responsibility, furthered this project. Positioning the practice near new home building, retail shopping, and heavy traffic patterns assured the future.

Most importantly, embracing computer technology has given the practice a huge advantage in accountability. With numbers crunched so quickly, I can be aware of trends or developments as they occur. Both in terms of treatment quality and in the mass of numbers that must be juggled, the EDO gives Gentle Dental an incredible edge. With the computer foundation in place, technical peripherals that are bound to occur can be tested and adopted far more easily. The practice thus gains an enviable flexibility.

These steps to quality—even though they serve my goal of building continuity—are no less important in your office than they are in mine.

CONCLUSION

Because I've made many mistakes, I invite you not to repeat them. What a waste of your time, talent, and resources that would be. Preventive measures are outlined. The caution is clear: Much of what happened to me can happen to anyone.

Since I've enjoyed considerable success with certain practice concepts, I invite you to consider testing, adopting, adapting, or improving them.

Size of practice never has been, isn't now, and never will be the goal. Bigness doesn't diminish the emphasis on our target, which forever is quality. The value of quality is the same in every dental practice.

I wish you Sooper days and half the fun in dentistry that I have had. Thank you for taking this trip with me.

DISSECTION LAB

After revealing my firsthand understanding of penury, we discussed the simple numbers that guide my overseeing GD. Weekly, they are production and new patient flow. Monthly, they are those two measures, plus front desk collections and accounts receivable over production. Infrequently, referral sources are tracked along with an analysis of accounts receivable.

A precaution not to overmanage was noted, as was the caution to respond when numbers don't match expectations.

In viewing goals, I observed that I generally think they warp the intention of seeking quality service for patients. The wrong emphasis misdirects office interest inward, rather than outward.

To succeed as a dental entrepreneur, if that is a goal, the dentist must be right-brain-oriented, with a willingness to risk and gamble and be creative.

My goal was to build a practice that would survive me—much like a Mayo Clinic, for example—which I defined through naming the practice with a generic name, hiring associates, and creating a business plan and a market aim. I noted the importance of hiring and training people who could be given responsibility to carry out the office plan.

Positioning the practice near new home building, heavy vehicular traffic, and retail shopping outlets was stressed. Finally, the critical computer capability was detailed.

There is never a substitute for quality.

APPENDIX A

---◆---

DOCTORS
WITH A HEART

In 1985, I took 12 ladies to lunch. There was a purpose. I needed their input and support for an idea that had been cooking in my mind for several years. I wanted to give a Valentine of thanks to the community for supporting Gentle Dental through good times and bad. The ladies were members of our staff/team. We had worked together for years, and they had protected me often.

Once, two of them called me into my office, told me to sit down and said, "Doctor, you are spending more time writing than you are with your patients. This is going to hurt the practice, and we'd like to see you take more interest in what goes on around here."

That's the kind of counsel good friends give good friends. I trusted these women. They've never let me down.

Even during days of our worst publicity—you've read the newspaper articles reprinted in this book—our business continued to grow and prosper. I think many people in the area viewed us as underdogs, and the world hates bullies.

"What if," I asked the ladies, "we closed our cash drawer and opened our hearts on Valentine's Day and gave away free dental service to people who have no money, no welfare, no job, no dental insurance. Anything we could do in one appointment, no questions asked. Would that work?"

Their answer was immediate and resounding. "Yes!" They loved the idea and we busied preparing a plan to carry out this day. There were two immediate concerns—what if too many people showed up and what if too few came to our party?

Some of the team planned for publicity. How do we get the word out to people who may not read the newspaper, listen to the radio, or watch television? They developed plans to spread the word through the council of churches, the Salvation Army, welfare agencies, and on 30-second, public-service spot announcements that we wrote and sent to the news media.

In-house planning meant rearranging furnishings to anticipate a large number of patients—worst-case-scenario planning. There would be no free coffee that day and more chairs packed into the reception room. A supplier gave us some X-ray film, alloy, and gloves. A grocer gave us juice and donuts for staff.

We had decided to open at 7 A.M. and run straight through until 5 P.M. We planned a party in the evening for all staff and spouses. All staff agreed to work without pay.

We decided we would offer prophylaxis, sealants, fluoride treatments, extractions, endodontics, operative, bonding, and repairs and relines for dentures. The basic services we offered would be anything we could do in one appointment. If we had too little response, we would do more for those in the chairs. If we had too many respondents, we would do less for each, but something for everyone.

As they arrived, patients were asked to sign a legal pad so we could serve them in order. A modified health questionnaire was devised for use that day, which would follow the patient through the system. One senior assistant was stationed in front to ask for the chief complaint and learn the patient's expectations.

She would then X-ray affected sites and refer the patient to the doctor or to hygiene for diagnosis and treatment. Patients were to sign informed consents, as usual. Nitrous oxide would not be available, because we believed it would slow the flow of traffic.

February 14, that year, dawned bitter cold and at 6:30 A.M. a dozen people shivered before our front door. "Let's get going, ladies and gentlemen," I said, and we brought the chilled patients into the warmth of our office and our hearts.

All day, a torrent of patients flooded through Gentle Dental. We had decided to let God do the screening, so if a person claimed to qualify, we assumed they were down on their luck and needed us.

One staffer asked me if I knew one old gentleman patient, who looked rather scruffy. I didn't, but she said she knew who he was. She revealed that he was a wealthy old recluse who owned a number of office buildings in town. Of course he didn't meet our qualifications, but we served him anyway.

I said to my staff informant, "Lisa, he's the poorest person we are serving today. Can you imagine how impoverished his soul must be, to cheat out someone truly in need of our free dental care?"

The day went incredibly well. Everyone pitched in and there was almost a festive feel in the air. Patients came for their important reasons, from pain to cosmetic need—to be more presentable for a job interview, for example.

That day we saw 170 patients and gave away more than $6,000 of free dental services. The day was the finest day of practice we ever had, and the staff had never been more of a team than that day. A unifying experience like that cannot be purchased.

The local television stations sent crews to film our event and to dominate the evening news. The newspaper featured our milestone on one entire page. The future of the happening was assured, for our giving came around so full force that we vowed never to miss another day like this—even without publicity.

When other dentists heard of the event, through an article in *Dental Economics,* we formed an organization called Doctors With A Heart. My daughter Cyd accepted the role of executive director and took over the nationwide job of telling other doctors how they could duplicate our day and replicate our happiness. Doctors of all stripes, from chiropractors to veterinarians, called to join the movement.

Everything you need to know to perform a like day in your practice is in this appendix that you have just read. Cyd quotes Proverbs 19:17 when people ask her about doing a DWAH day. The verse goes, "When you help the poor you are lending to the Lord . . . and He pays wonderful interest on your loan."

It could not be better said.

APPENDIX B

---◆---

INFORMED CONSENTS, RELEASES, REFUSALS, RECOMMENDATIONS, AND WARRANTIES

The following documents perform two functions—they remind us to inform before we perform and they bear witness that information was given. Never fail to request the document and never fail to record the patient's signature or failure to sign.

When the patient refuses to sign, a decision must be made. For example, if they refuse to sign a release upon receiving a refund, odds grow that they contemplate legal action. Believe it or not, I have given a refund which was used to hire a lawyer to sue me. Now that's the height of stupidity—mine. Never again.

Some patients may refuse to sign an informed consent for a procedure, which brings up decision time again. Generally, if they refuse to sign because I merely told them bad things could happen, then I figure they must have an agenda that I would as soon not be part of. We invite those people out of the practice, telling them we will help them find another dentist.

If a patient refuses to sign because he won't give up his right to sue, I tell him he is not giving up his right to redress if we do him wrong. Arbitration will care for him and treat him fairly. In thousands of times that this pledge has been signed, only one gentleman objected. After I explained that he would not lose his right to settlement if we failed to follow the standards, he signed.

If a patient refuses X-rays or medications, again decision time is upon us. For an extraction, I don't believe extracting a tooth in the absence of an X-ray can be justified as equal to the standard of care. I would invite that patient out of the practice, give him or her a prescription, and help find a dentist who might do that procedure.

If holding the X-ray in the mouth is a problem, there are extra-oral techniques that work reasonably well enough to satisfy the situation.

A patient who refuses medication is another challenge. Generally, we check with the physician if, for example, a patient has had childhood rheumatic fever and has never been premedicated for the risk of subacute bacterial endocarditis. With a physician's approval, in cases of heart disease, parts replacements, and former disease—each of which might normally result in premedication precautions—we will go ahead and work for the unprotected patient. We ask them to sign a release, however, to protect us.

Signing a release for refusing a treatment plan is more window dressing than anything else. Sometimes it brings patients up short to realize they are putting themselves at risk for failing to follow our recommendations. Reassessment sometimes brings acquiescence. Often not. We have the treatment plan on file, the X-rays, and tooth and perio charts, and witnesses that know the patient refused. He probably first refused treatment to a chairside assistant, so he believes the program is between him and her, rather than him and me.

Once more I point out, the binding arbitration clause that we print in our informed consents and new patient registry has not been tested in any court that I know of. If it ever is, and if it is upheld, I have a signed document on every single GD patient going back for several years. Upheld or not, it is a comfort to have these signatures.

Finally, never destroy an informed consent. After the statute of limitations has expired, microfilm the batch and then recycle the paper.

Here are the documents we employ. Check them with your attorney for applicability to your state dental practice act and to your state code. Except for the first text, the binding arbitration clause is not reprinted each time.

INFORMED CONSENT
FOR TOOTH EXTRACTIONS

A few years ago, I wanted to standardize informed consent presentations. The easiest way to do that is to put a presentation on film. A generic extraction film was created with professional photographers and models. The film lasts two minutes and 20 seconds and is illustrated with drawings. We show this film to every person, prior to an extraction.

In response to the need for a series of videotaped informed consents, a series has been scripted and filmed and is available through PennWell Dental Books. When you will be called into court to tell a jury what you told your patient prior to the procedure for which he is now suing you, it will be your word against his. Juries have believed patients over doctors many times.

Now consider showing the jury the same film your aggrieved patient saw. They will believe *your film* every time. The full protection afforded by filmed informed consents doesn't cost what your professional liability insurance costs for a month. Yet the shield of safety it gives you can be the difference between tragedy and triumph. Following the film, the patient signs this document:

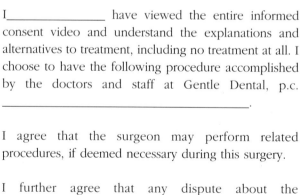

I_____ have viewed the entire informed consent video and understand the explanations and alternatives to treatment, including no treatment at all. I choose to have the following procedure accomplished by the doctors and staff at Gentle Dental, p.c.

_____.

I agree that the surgeon may perform related procedures, if deemed necessary during this surgery.

I further agree that any dispute about the reasonableness or computation of fees, or any claim of negligent or intentional acts or omissions in the rendering of professional services, either in this instance or in any other treatment rendered by staff in this office, *shall be submitted to binding arbitration under Chapter 679A of the Code of Iowa (1993). It is understood by both doctors and patient that by agreeing to submit all claims or assertions that either patient or doctor may have against the other, arising out of this agreement, patient and doctors have given up their right to a jury or court trial.*

Signed, Witnessed, Dated

(The portion in italic type is the portion under question and unresolved by the courts on this date of publication.)

Other informed consents follow the same pattern. Be sure that any patient, including best-friend patients, sign a release for every procedure. These requirements are no more optional than are gloves, anesthetic, or financial arrangements.

OTHER RECOMMENDED CONSENTS

1. Informed Consent for Precision Crowns & Bridges

2. Informed Consent for Periodontal Surgery

3. Informed Consent for Root Canal Treatment

4. Informed Consent for Dental Surgical Procedure

5. Informed Consent for Alveoplasty

Several documents require signatures that, while not strictly informed consents, are dentist-protective. Do not fail to have every involved patient sign these documents, as well.

Refuse X-ray

I have been advised that the following X-ray(s) are now due for my dental health, as prescribed by my dentist at Gentle Dental, p.c.

- Bitewing X-rays for decay and disease detection
- Periapical X-ray for root examination
- Panoramic X-ray for disease detection

I have chosen not to have these X-rays taken and accept full consequences for failing to have them. I will not hold doctor and staff at Gentle Dental responsible for any adverse circumstance that occurs to me for having failed to have the prescribed X-rays taken.

Signed, witnessed, dated

Refuse Medication

I have been advised that premedication is the standard of care for people with my medical history. The risks of not taking this premedication have been explained to me; and I understand that they include, but may not be limited to, loss of a prosthetic replacement, serious infections in body organs including the heart, and that symptoms and disease, including death, are possible months from now.

I acknowledge that these risks have been explained to me and that I have no further questions regarding them. (Arbitration paragraph)

Signed, witnessed, dated

Refuse Treatment Plan

I release the doctors and staff at Gentle Dental due to my failure to accept a treatment plan that was designed for me and thoroughly explained. By refusing to accept this plan I understand that my dental health will be compromised and will deteriorate.

My questions have been answered and I feel comfortable with my decision. (Arbitration paragraph)

Signed, witnessed, dated

Denture Limited Warranty

I understand that Gentle Dental cannot guarantee that my new denture will work the way I want it to. It has been explained to me, and I understand, that jaws differ, people differ, and denture results can be unpredictable.

I further understand that GD will adjust the denture they make for me, for life, without charge. This, once again, does not imply or mean that I will ever feel the denture works as well as I expect.

I will pay one-half the fee at the impression and one-half before I receive the denture. (Arbitration paragraph)

Signed, witnessed, dated

Denture Repair Limited Warranty

I understand that Gentle Dental cannot guarantee that plastic will not break, or break again, including the plastic that is broken prior to this repair. I agree to accept the best efforts of the technicians, staff, and doctors at Gentle Dental and to not hold them liable in the event this denture breaks again, even if it breaks again today.

Release Following Refund

For the sole consideration of $_____, I _____, and my heirs, forever discharge the doctors, staff, and Gentle Dental, p.c. from any and all claims which I may have at any time due to the incursion of this debt.

It is understood that the repayment of these funds is not to be construed as an admission of liability. (Arbitration paragraph)

Signed, witnessed, dated

Recommend Arbitration

Dear _____:

We have reviewed your request for refund for services rendered at Gentle Dental, p.c. and feel that the service and fee were appropriate to the need.

Since we have agreed to binding arbitration, in accord with the document you signed at the inception of this service, we suggest the arbitrator (company/person) of _____, whose normal fee for this will be $ ____ . According to the terms of our agreement, we will pay half this fee and you will be obligated for the other half.

If you wish to pursue this matter, please make your check payable to _____ (the arbitrator). When payment has been made, the arbitrator can gather facts and render a decision.

APPENDIX C

---◆---

THE STAFF
MISSION MANUAL

GENTLE DENTAL, PC
THE OFFICE MANUAL

TABLE OF CONTENTS

From time to time, a Gentle Dental (GD) employee may be asked to perform duties other than those for which they were originally hired. It is understood that team members will willingly help out where management decides that the employee's talents and skills may be best employed, consistent with the needs of the office, both in terms of time and regarding specific duties.

"What you see here and hear here stays here when you leave here."

THE GENTLE DENTAL TEAM

1. GOAL

A team works together and pulls together, all teammates working toward the same goal. The purpose of this manual is to invite you to be part of our team, pull in the direction we are headed, and enjoy our mutual goals. In his landmark book, *The 7 Habits of Highly Effective People,* Stephen Covey states: "A team knows which way is North." We own the compass.

At GD our entire mission statement is two words long: Have Fun!

That's all there is to it, because life and work and relationships were designed to be enjoyable. Having fun includes all the other words from all other mission statements.

Substandard work is no fun. Not delivering the greatest possible dental experience is no fun. Not learning on the job, not respecting each other, not lending a helping hand is no fun.

It's no fun when we're not given the tools with which to grow. When we're not rewarded fairly for a job well done, it's no darn fun. We are going to have fun and those who don't want to will be wished well on their next job.

We want your suggestions, after you have committed this book to memory. Each team member must know this book, must promise to uphold and follow GD procedures, and must agree to promptly report any variations from our theme. We're all going North!

Another way that our goal could be stated would be to say that we will provide quality health care promptly, and affordable fees, through superb dental experiences, with no discrimination for age, race, religion, skin color, national origin, sex, sexual preference, income or occupation. "Have Fun" still says it all.

2. STAFF CODE

High professional standards of conduct for all members of the team set our group apart both inside and outside the office. When a teammate dishonors this creed outside the office, it reflects poorly on all.

Inside the office we work together in a spirit of harmonious cooperation. In a few words: We give each other the benefit of the doubt and we know that no matter how thinly bread is sliced, there are always two sides to each slice.

At GD, we afford each other the respect of hearing both sides before drawing a conclusion.

3. PUNCTUALITY

When a person is late they impose on others and that is, in one word, rude. Tardiness is an unacceptable form of behavior.

4. ATTITUDE

People who live negative lives suffer more sickness and have more accidents. They have fewer friends, earn less, die sooner, and cannot achieve the GD goal of Having Fun! Negatives destroy and are not allowed.

5. RESTRICTIVE ILLNESS

Please do not work on any day you have signs or symptoms of contagious illness. We don't want each others bugs, do we?

6. SEXUAL HARASSMENT

No. Not by suggestion, not by remark, not by look, not by deed, not by action, not by posted nonsense. None.

7. DRESS CODE

Look professional. That's what professional dental assistants, hygienists, and doctors do. And that's us! We wear uniforms to present a uniformly fine appearance. Tops under gowns must not show beneath the gown.

Here's some basic no's: No strong perfumes, no exotic or showy jewelry, no heavy aftershaves, no weird nail designs, no wild hairdos, no skirts, no sloppy jeans, no sandals, no shorts, no chewing gum, no food, snacks, or beverages at any work station. No uniformed staffer may enter the lounge area.

Hair must be tied back. Name tags are to be worn at all times. Smiles are required on all faces.

8. PROFESSIONAL EDUCATION

Learning is a never-ending task. Pro athletes work out daily. Professional musicians practice daily. Professional actors constantly work to improve their craft. You are a pro.

CPR certifications and recertifications are provided free for all staff and required for staff involved in direct patient care. OSHA education is provided free and required. X-ray certification and recertification is required of chairside staff and provided free. Monthly staff meetings and other educational experiences, including on the job training (OJT) are provided as well, and attendance is required.

9. WORK SCHEDULE

The Office Administrator (OA) will work with staff to create work schedules. Every effort is made to match office needs with staff wants. It cannot always be a perfect match. The OA's decision shall be final.

No staff member may change her schedule, or swap time slots with another staff member, without the OA's approval at least a day before the swap is to take place.

10. A SECOND JOB

The Bible says a person cannot serve two masters as he will serve only one and neglect the other. Full-time employees will find this to be a full-time job. A second job is unacceptable.

11. TELEPHONE USEAGE

The telephone brings us work. No personal calls are permitted during working hours. Personal calls will be saved for you. You may return them if you have a break, or during lunch break, only after you log out.

When making any call, do not seize the last available line. We must be able to accept all incoming calls. Patients may only use the special patient line in reception room. No patient may use our business phone.

12. TRIAL BASIS

All employees are hired for a three-month trial period. During this time you may quit if you find that this job is not for you. GD may also dismiss, if it is decided your talents do not match the job. Neither you, nor GD, is required to give a reason for quitting or for dismissing any employee.

13. HEPTAVAX

Employees who qualify for Category I or II status (as determined by OSHA, for persons who could be exposed to bloodborne pathogens) are offered the Heptavax series (three shots over six months) for immunity to Hepatitis.

The new employee may decline; however, they may later accept, up until six months before they give notice. Hepatitis shots given to employees who do not stay for the entire series will be deducted from their final check.

14. RADIOGRAPHS

Unless certified by the Iowa Board of Dental Examiners, no staff member may take patient X-rays. A student status may be obtained and the costs of certification will be borne by GD.

15. RADIATION

All staff members who work near radiation shall be tested each quarter (every three months). The staff member will wear and develop their own film badge and this will be placed in their employment file.

Only a patient may occupy a room in which a film is exposed. Staff must be outside the room to activate the button.

16. EYE PROTECTION

During cutting procedures, all patients, chairside staff, and doctors must wear eye-protective devices. Eyewash stations and chemical eyewash solutions are available. Their locations must be known before working in these areas during these procedures.

17. HAZARDOUS CHEMICALS

There are many chemicals employed in GD procedures. Those who work with them must know their dangers, antidotes, and precautionary handling measures.

Material Safety Data Sheets (MSDS) are located in a well-marked binder and available when needed. Know where they are. In the event of a mishap, a GD dentist must be notified at once.

18. EXPOSURE INCIDENTS

There are not two ways to handle an exposure incident. You are required by law to know what to do in this event. There is one and only one way to handle an exposure incident and this is it:

1. Notify a doctor at once. Another chairside will replace you when you tell her what happened.

2. MAKE IT BLEED!

3. Wash the area and apply hydrogen peroxide or alcohol.

4. Obtain a "Red Card" from the front desk, call the hospital emergency room, and go there at once. GD uses St. Luke's Hospital in these emergencies.

5. By 4:30 that afternoon (or between 7–7:30 the following morning) set up an appointment with the St. Luke's Occupational Healthcare Center.

Guess what's easier and $175 cheaper? Don't have an exposure incident in the first place. If you have followed our protocols, an exposure incident will not happen.

19. ACCIDENTS ON THE JOB

All accidents must be immediately reported to someone—the doctor, the Exposure Control Manager, the OA, fellow staff members. Don't wing it! Simply tell someone and we will help you, at once. We're a team. Remember?

20. STERILITY REGIMENS

We know how to sterilize stuff, and you must, too. That's why we teach you these procedures first (if you are chairside). Face masks, gloves of all sizes and descriptions, gowns and face shields, we've got it all. Our office has been denoted as the first dental office in the world to meet every single standard for a bloodborne pathogen defense. Don't let yourself down by violating that standard.

21. PAYROLL DEDUCTIONS

We allow as many as you wish and our computers won't forget. Just tell us. Those most used are credit union, office trip, and insurances. No problem.

22. DENTAL CARE

A great GD benefit that only has a couple of strings. If you leave during the year following dental care, you will be charged the cost of the care from your last paycheck or benefit check. No exceptions. While routine dental care is free, crowns, bridges, and dentures are half price.

Your immediate family—husband, wife, and children only—receive dental care at 50 percent off. Mother, father, sister, and brother receive care at 25 percent off. Other relatives, such as inlaws and outlaws, do not receive a discount. If an employee has dental insurance, dental care will be delivered and processed through the insurance carrier.

23. PAID HOLIDAYS

Six holidays are recognized: New Year's Day, Memorial Day, Independence Day, Labor Day, Thanksgiving Day, and Christmas Day.

Full-time employees—that is, those who work at least 35 hours weekly, and have done so the past 6 months—will be paid a salary for that day if the day falls on a regular work day for them. One may not trade days to obtain a holiday-pay day.

24. VACATIONS

During the first 12 months, an employee earns four hours of paid vacation per month.

During the second through the fifth year, the employee earns eight hours per month. This is the equivalent of two weeks and two days of paid vacation.

From the sixth year on, the employee earns 10 hours paid vacation per month. This is the equivalent of three weeks paid vacation.

Several rules:

1. Vacation time must be applied for three weeks in advance.

2. Vacation days are allotted on the basis of seniority.

3. Unpaid vacation days off may be arranged, in advance.

4. No vacation and work pay for the same day allowed.

5. No vacation days allowed during the time when a staff member gives notice.

6. Vacations are allotted so that enough staff remains to continue office operations.

7. Vacation pay is awarded the payday following.

25. SICKNESS/HEALTH INSURANCE

There is no sick pay. If you call in ill, you must talk with a staff member, not the answering service, and please do not leave a message. An excuse from a physician is required for repeated sick calls, as needed and determined by the OA.

Full-time employees (35-40 hours weekly) qualify for health insurance benefits. A base maximum is allowed and costs over that are borne by the employee.

When a spouse has the opportunity to gain health insurance, the employee may not have GD health insurance. Exceptions may be made, allowing the employee to buy GD health care coverage through a deduction plan when this does not incur extra cost. Upon being accepted by the insurance company for coverage, a waiting period of 60 days prevails.

26. GOVERNMENT PROGRAMS

Social Security, Worker's Compensation, Unemployment Compensation, and Medicaid coverage are deductibles paid for all GD employees, in addition to deductions for state and federal income taxes.

When an employee is dismissed, GD will dispute unemployment compensation claims.

27. SALARIES

Payday is every other Friday, all year long. Thursday evening is the cutoff day. Several rules apply:

1. No overtime is allowed. None. This is an absolute and violators will be relieved of their time card. (The U.S. Department of Commerce requires overtime pay but we do not allow overtime to accrue.)

2. Lunch breaks must be at least 30 minutes. (U.S. Department of Commerce rule)

3. Log-in time is 10 minutes before your shift and only 10 minutes before your shift. Excessive log-in times will be deducted from pay.

A 10-minute break during a long shift may be allowed and may not. The sole determination is the doctor and the patient flow. A break during work schedule is not a law, nor does the U.S. Department of Commerce require any breaks at all. No more than two assistants at a time may break.

28. SMOKING

GD is smoke-free. That includes the parking lot, outside the doors, and about anywhere you can be seen smoking. Do it anywhere you wish, but not at GD. Staff smokers send really bad health messages to the patients we serve.

29. CREDIT UNION

GD belongs to First Federal Commercial Credit Union and staff members may join and have payroll savings deductions made. The credit union also provides other credit services such as ATM cards, loans, share drafts, and various savings instruments.

30. STAFF LOUNGE

Vending machines, a refrigerator, and a microwave are provided for staff meals. No cooking before 11:30 A.M. That's an absolute rule. No friends or relatives may visit the staff lounge area. It is reserved solely for staff's private use.

31. VISITORS

None allowed behind the scenes. This goes for the operatories, labs, staff lounge, doctors' offices, and business offices. Entertain your friends everywhere except at GD. This is a serious health care facility, not a casual shop. Friends may wait for you for short periods of time in the north reception room only.

32. EMPLOYEE PARKING

Lighted employee parking is only available in designated spaces. Learn them and use them. Our most convenient spaces are always reserved for the "boss" . . . our patient.

33. FINANCIAL ARRANGEMENTS

Learn them, use them, and then never worry if there's money in the bank to pay your salary. GD has never missed a payroll, and we are not about to start. The reason is simple: we inform before we perform.

34. HIV+/AIDS PATIENTS

All GD infection-barrier techniques currently in place protect everyone, perfectly. Many of these patients will not tell us they carry these viruses. It doesn't matter. Not one dental employee, hygienist, or dentist has ever contacted AIDS from a patient in a dental office.

If you learn a patient is HIV+, you may discuss it only with the treating dentist, not one other human being in or out of the office.

If you violate this federal law, you will be immediately dismissed, and possibly sued by the patient. He will probably win a large settlement, and no insurance in the world will protect you. These are hard facts, but this is a political disease. That's all the warning you get.

35. IMPRESSION TECHNIQUES

Only doctors may take all final impressions. Staff may take opposing arch impressions, bite registrations, and study model impressions. That's all.

36. TEMPORARY CROWNS

All temporary crowns, by Iowa law, must be placed by the doctor. The assistant may fabricate the crown outside the mouth.

37. QUARTERLY RELEASE

Every three months, all staff members are required to sign a document that states that they have:

1. Neither witnessed nor engaged in any sexual harassment at GD;

2. Neither witnessed nor engaged in any illegal acts performed by dental asistants;

3. Neither witnessed nor engaged in any illegal billing; and

4. Agree to binding arbitration in the event of any labor dispute.

38. CONDITIONAL EMPLOYMENT AGREEMENT

I understand that I am employed for a trial period of three months. This does not constitute full-time employment, qualifying for unemployment benefits. I can be dismissed at any time, with no reason given. I may quit at any time, without giving a reason.

Dental Care: I agree to the terms of this employee manual and, if needed, will repay GD either from my last paycheck as a deduction or from my pocket, if payment is due.

Health Insurance Agreement: If health insurance is in effect, it will continue only through the month of my departure.

Infection Barrier Control: I agree to learn and immediately abide by all techniques in effect at GD. I will promptly learn cross-contamination control and how to handle biohazardous materials, where the MSDS sheets are and how to use them, and how to deal with exposure incidents and, more importantly, how to avoid them.

I agree to the ADA, CDC, and OSHA requirements and will view appropriate tapes and documents to learn the current status for my position.

Rules: I agree to all the rules as set forth in this document.

I authorize a reference check of those names I submitted and a credit check, as well as a check of any police record.

I do not currently suffer from, nor have I had in the past, any known infectious agents that may cause tuberculosis, venereal diseases, HIV+/AIDS, and/or hepatitis.

I understand GD allows appropriate maternity leave, as may be required, without penalty. I understand that GD will ask for my dismissal from a call for jury duty because of my importance in the health care field.

I agree that this employment agreement may be terminated at will, with or without cause, with or without notice, at any time, at either my option or at the option of GD.

Signed_____ Dated_____

Witness _____ Dated_____

APPENDIX D

◆

DENTAL INTERNET RESOURCES

DENTAL RESOURCES ON THE INTERNET

Access The University of Iowa College of Dentistry Home Page and follow the links to all the Dentistry links known!

The easy way: type in the URL (this stands for Uniform Resource Locator; think of it as an address): `http://www.uiowa.edu/` for The University of Iowa Homepage, follow this link to **Academic Programs** then the link to **College of Dentistry Home Page**.

You can directly access the College's Home Page by using a direct URL: `http://indy.radiology.uiowa.edu/Beyond/Dentistry/DentistryHP.html` Scroll to the bottom of the Home Page and link to other Internet Dentistry sites.

On the College's Home Page, you will find:

◆ information for patients
◆ information for students
◆ information for health professionals, including Continuing Education
◆ College of Dentistry Directory
◆ other Internet Dental resources

Some other **URL's** for you:

Glossary of Internet terms	`http://www.matisse.net/files/glossary.html`
Beginner's Luck	`http://www.execpc.com/~wmhogg/beginner.html`
Awesome List	`http://www.clark.net/pub/journalism/awesome.html`
ElNet Galaxy	`http://galaxy.einet.net/galaxy.html`
Web Guide	`http://www.mecklerweb.com/webguide/entry.htm`
Guide to Cyberspace	`http://www.eit.com/web/www.guide/`
Dental-X-Change	`http://odont.com/index.htm`

For more information, please contact:

`janice-quinn@uiowa.edu`

`lynn-johnson@uiowa.edu`

APPENDIX E

❖

TAKING CARE
OF BUSINESS

The orderly conduct of commerce requires rules, and the profession of dentistry is not excused from this business requirement. Office rules decide how the practice is to be run, but since we own the show, we get to decide which rules to follow. It works that way everywhere in business.

For example, restaurants bar patrons from entering the kitchen. Smokers cannot sit among nonsmokers. Customers are forbidden entrance into automobile service bays. We cannot board an airplane until we are invited. The movie theater empties before it refills for the next showing.

There are millions more. People may be charged with abandonment if they leave an untended child in a department store. When customers break an item that they mishandled, they will be charged for it. Grocers require payment at the checkout counter. Most proprietors require their customers to wear a shirt and shoes.

Some examples from health care: Family and friends are barred from surgical operating rooms. People who refuse to give medical history information are refused medical treatment. Visiting hours are episodic. People who fail to sign consent forms are denied treatment.

In a move to reduce customer confrontation with their rules, business owners often shift blame to a nameless third party. For example: "Our accountant requires . . . ," "The FAA insists . . . ," "Your insurance company demands . . . ," "Federal law forbids . . . ," "OSHA has ruled . . . ," and "The Standard of Care that we are held to does not allow . . .".

The cost is high to dentists who fail to establish strict rules and teach staff to enforce them. The price to those doctors comes in the form of stress, fatigue, and burnout. Conversely, a disciplined office, operating under thoughtful policies, achieves nice profits in the form of a happier staff, less stress, reduced fatigue, more peaceful days, more control of one's destiny, greater job security, and earlier retirement. Need more?

In an earlier chapter, we noted how barriers can keep patients out of our chairs. Selective screening will also weed and wean patients, too, but that's not all bad. In most dental offices, if certain troublesome patients were lost to the practice, staff would rejoice. Patients who break appointments, who are obstreperous or obnoxious or, worse yet, who are litigant-prone, are not the kind of people we want to do business with anyway.

The following business elements guide our practice and contribute to a good work environment. You may want to consider adopting or adapting some of them to your operations. Here are the Gentle Dental barriers that we teach our staff.

COPING WITH THE UNUSUAL AT GENTLE DENTAL

Gentle Dental conducts a private practice of dentistry. That means we have the right to choose whom we will serve and to exclude whom we wish. Since it is illegal to stop halfway through a procedure, we should be certain we will finish the treatments that we begin.

Reaching that certainty is why we screen patients for health reasons. A patient whose medical condition is too severely compromised may be referred to a dental facility better able to deal with his condition. We screen our patients for their wants through examination, diagnosis, and treatment plan presentations. Patients whose wants cannot be elevated to the level of their needs then may screen themselves from further care, at least for the moment.

Financial planning before treatment begins further screens patients to assure that those filling our chairs are willing to meet their financial obligation in a timely and acceptable manner. A patient who has papered the town with unmet bills, has been turned over to collection, has undergone bankruptcy, or has his charge cards filled to the maximum, must live by certain of our rules that protect our business future.

Patients are screened for behavior and for assurance that they will accept the rules we define for the work environment we fashion. They must accept all our rules in terms of the standard of care that we deliver, and also in matters of dress, decency, and conduct. We want the assurance that they are people we truly want to work for.

At GD, we once dismissed a patient from the practice because he showed for his appointment in work clothes. Many people, of course, wear work attire to a dental appointment, but this fellow's job made a big difference. He worked in a rendering works and from 50 feet away every nose was offended. After his first visit we had to carry on major fumigation procedures. When we requested that he shower and change before his next appointment, he angrily left the practice.

Of course, we do not reject patients on the basis of race, religion, gender, sexual orientation, or health status (meaning primarily AIDS and HIV+ patients). We welcome patients who accept our diagnosis and treatment plans, who make and keep financial arrangements, who show for their appointments, and who follow our rules. Those who will not, are invited to leave the practice.

There is only one minor exception. We practice with compassion. A patient who has a serious urgency will not be denied emergency dental care, even though we know at the outset we may not be compensated for the effort. Everything in life cannot carry a price tag, and our empathy for people who have suffered misfortune—self-induced or beyond their control—is one aspect of our practice that falls outside the profit motive. Those who screen our callers need to know that rule.

This document will be your guide to handling the unusual situation that occurs. It is important that you learn these responses. If you meet a circumstance that stumps you for a response, put the patient on hold and seek help from a senior staff member. Then listen, observe, and learn how to handle the problem.

Whatever you do, please do not wing it, make up your own rules, or guess at an answer. The consequences can be severe, both to the practice and to you, for we conduct a business that must operate under literally thousands of federal, state, local, and dental laws. The responses put forth in this chapter are tested and proven proper, so you are always on safe ground when you follow these guidelines. Those who make up their own answers tread treacherous waters.

Patient Problem Number 1:
A patient complains about a doctor.

Action to take: Smile, look the patient in the eye, and say: "Thank you for telling me."

Then, only if you judge that it is appropriate: "Would you like to be appointed with another Gentle Dental doctor?" Alternate answer: "I'll be sure the doctor knows of your comment." Note, you said "comment," not "complaint."

- Show the patient you care.

- Try to define the specific complaint. Talk with the patient, and more importantly, listen to what he says.

- Make clear and complete notes about the complaint in the patient's ledger, using his words, as much as you can.

- Inform the Office Administrator (OA) and the Doctor, ASAP.

What not to do:

- Do not agree with the patient.

- Do not promise any relief.

- Do not promise anything, including when someone will deal with the patient's comment.

A kind word often turns away anger. Your role is to be sympathetic, without agreeing. If you agree, you make a judgment call that you are not in a position to make.

Do not argue with the patient or defend the situation. It would be all right to say, "I'm very surprised. Doctor has pleased so many patients."

Exactly what did the patient not like about the care he or she received? Try to find a specific reason. Sympathize with the patient without agreeing. You have no idea whether this is a legitimate complaint or not. The patient may be gathering fuel to file a lawsuit. He may merely want out of paying his bill. He may merely be having a "bad hair" day.

Your role, as the GD employee hearing the complaint—whether you are a chairside assistant, business assistant, lab technician, hygienist, or doctor, either on-duty or off-duty—is to gather as many clear facts as possible, record them, and see that the doctor and the OA both know of the complaint. The office must respond in some fashion.

Actions for you to take:

- Make a complete note in the patient's file.

- Inform both the doctor and the OA in the computer mailbox file. Your responsibility then ends and you get an 'A' grade. Complaints about other staff members are handled in the same fashion.

Actions for the office to take:

- Doctor may wish to call the patient and possibly apologize, or offer the services of another doctor. The doctor may decide it is best that no doctor call be made.

- The office administrator will then call. Someone must and will respond.

PATIENT PROBLEM NUMBER 2:
PATIENT SWEARS, MAKES SEXUALLY EXPLICIT SUGGESTIONS OR ADVANCES, OR APPEARS INTOXICATED OR DRUGGED.

No Gentle Dental employee will tolerate any improper behavior by any patient. There are no exceptions.

Actions to take:

TELEPHONE ABUSE

When a patient swears or becomes abusive, simply say, "I'm sorry sir (or madam)," and hang up. Period. Do not listen anymore and do not argue or criticize the patient. Simply cradle the receiver.

If the abusive person calls back, and you learn who it is, tell the caller that you will visit with him or her about the problem only if there is no profanity. If the caller refuses to behave properly, refuse the call. Make complete notes, including the exact words used. These notes may serve an attorney well, if this confrontation escalates into a lawsuit.

Continued calls of harassment should be immediately reported to the OA or to a senior doctor on duty. The telephone company may monitor abusive callers. In extreme cases, the police will deal with telephone harassment.

The important point to remember is that the office backs you and your actions over any patient's claim. We trust and believe in our own staff and will not tolerate abusive patients.

CHAIRSIDE ABUSE

When a patient becomes profane, abusive, makes sexually explicit or suggestive remarks, or tries to touch an assistant, do not deal with the patient. Leave the chair at once and inform a doctor. The doctor will handle the circumstance.

The doctor may ask the patient to correct his or her behavior, and in the event the patient refuses, the doctor may dismiss the patient from the practice, at once. The doctor may decide to dismiss the patient, without giving an opportunity to correct the behavior.

A strapping GD patient once tried to put his elbow onto the hygienist's lap, during his prophylaxis. At once, she wisely left the chair and reported the incident. When I called him on his behavior, he apologized profusely and I believed him. He was told our staff would continue to work for him but that he would be on probation. For the past 15 years he has been an exemplary patient, and has now become a good practice friend. I suppose we should lift the probation.

Upon being alerted to a problem patient, the doctor may tell the patient, "We do not accept this behavior from our patients and, if you wish, I will help you find another dentist." The doctor will then usher the patient from the practice.

Granted, these are extreme and rare instances, but they have occurred in the past and will again in the future. Make complete ledger notes to record each event.

No doctor will work on a patient who smells of alcohol or appears to be on drugs. These patients may be dismissed from the appointment and may be asked to return in a sober state, or may be dismissed from the practice with no opportunity for reprieve. The decision to dismiss patients temporarily or permanently is solely the doctor's.

PATIENT PROBLEM NUMBER 3:
PATIENT ARRIVES IMPROPERLY DRESSED FOR AN APPOINTMENT.

Action to take: "No shirt, no shoes, no service" works in grocery stores, restaurants, and department stores. The same rule serves GD. At check-in, the receptionist should perceive the problem and ask the patient to leave and return properly attired.

"Sorry, but we have the same rule that (name a local chain restaurant) has."

The patient may have the time or inclination to go home and get properly attired and still keep the appointment, or not. That's the patient's problem. We accept nothing less and make no apology for our rules. This general rule is universal enough to not need posting. If there is a problem, always call a doctor to the scene.

PATIENT PROBLEM NUMBER 4:
PATIENT ARRIVES FOR APPOINTMENT WITH INFANTS IN TOW OR IN ARMS.
THE CHILDREN OBVIOUSLY MUST BE TENDED DURING THE APPOINTMENT.

Action to take: "I'm sorry, but our insurance does not allow children in the operatory."

If the patient protests he or she has brought children in the past into the operatory, say, "These are new rules and we have no choice." Smile (smiles always help solve problems, don't they?) and say, "We don't make the rules."

If they have been allowed in the operatory in the past, it is possible that the doctor may make a one-time exception, establishing with the parent that this cannot recur. GD is a dental office, not a child care center. Always make complete ledger notes.

Imagine an untended child coming into contact with a bloodborne pathogen in our operatory. Imagine the horror of a child, or an infant in a basket, being accidentally blinded with a formo-cresol spill or with a fallen sharps, or a flying tooth particle. Those awful potentials are real. We refuse to be a party to such irresponsibility. There are no exceptions.

PATIENT PROBLEM NUMBER 5: PARENT WANTS TO GO TO THE OPERATORY WITH THEIR CHILD.

(The reverse of Problem 4) This category may include patients who want another person to "babysit" them or hold their hand during the dental appointment.

Action to take: "I'm sorry but our insurance allows only patients and employees in the operatory."

If a patient protests, say: "I'm sorry, but I have no choice. I don't make the rules."

The doctor may decide the parent may stand in the operatory doorway and observe, as long as the child is unaware that the parent is within squalling distance.

The doctor may say something like, "Caring for your child is too important for me to accept needless and pointless risk. We work with sharp instruments and a sudden movement or distraction could result in harm to your child. I'm here to help him, not hurt him. And I help him best when we let him grow, through handling the dental appointment on his own."

PATIENT PROBLEM NUMBER 6: PATIENT REFUSES TO SIGN THE ADMITTING DOCUMENT THAT ATTESTS TO THE ACCURACY OF HIS HEALTH HISTORY, ASSIGNS INSURANCE BENEFITS, GIVES PERMISSION TO CHECK HIS CREDIT, AND AGREES TO BINDING ARBITRATION, FOREGOING HIS RIGHT TO SUE.

Action to take: Smile, learn exactly which aspect of his signature he objects to, and say, "We have never treated a patient who has failed to sign this document so let me get someone who can answer your questions."

You continue, "While I'm finding someone to visit with you, this explanation may answer your questions." As he reads, find a senior receptionist, the OA, or a doctor. Be sure to hand the patient the correct explanation for his problem. If he objected to signing a health history, the paragraph you hand him will say:

> The standard of care of proper dental practice requires a signed health history, prior to seeing a patient. The law allows no exceptions. We cannot treat any patient who refuses this state requirement.

If the patient objected to the credit check, the copy will state:

> Our accountant requires a credit check on all patients who may need deferred payment plans. There is no cost to you. We have found that people with good credit do not mind this normal business function. Since we do not know your needs, and the proposed costs, and your choice of payment method, we require the permission to check credit.

If the patient persists in not allowing a credit check, refer to a senior receptionist or the OA. There are situations where we may wave this requirement, but those judgment calls must be made by senior staff.

When a patient refuses to assign insurance benefits, he will usually do so with something like, "I'll fill out my own insurance and submit it and they can pay me directly." Having been through that problem many times—waiting while patients collected payment and we did not—we simply refuse this denial.

This is a two-way street. On the patient's side, we accept insurance assignment as payment in full and only require that the patient pay the patient portion, at the time of service. On our side, we must have assignment or payment in full by the patient at the time of service. He cannot have it both ways.

If a patient refuses to agree to arbitration and give up his right to a jury trial, we again hold fast. A patient who fails to agree to arbitration may have another plan in mind. We do not wish to be a part of those plans for they will not serve the best interests of this office.

The card you hand him, while you obtain senior assistance to fend his objection, will read:

> Arbitration is the modern way to protect people's rights. Arbitration agreements are used today by most insurance companies, banks, stock brokers, and even lawyers. If you ever should happen to have a grievance with this office, over the standard of care or billing, we want to be fair and we agree to abide by the decision of an unbiased arbitrator. This system is fair, personal, prompt, and simple, and neither you, nor this office, has given up the right to fair settlement.

This same card is available in the operatories for patients who may refuse to sign an informed consent form, all of which contains the same agreement to arbitration. Mention might be made of the fact that we have employed this statement more than 10,000 times, without a single objection.

PATIENT PROBLEM NUMBER 7:
A CALLER ASKS FOR THE FULL NAME, ADDRESS, OR TELEPHONE NUMBER OF A STAFF MEMBER OR A DOCTOR.

Never. Never give out personal data on any employee. A caller may plead that the hygienist (receptionist, assistant, or doctor) was so nice that he now merely wants to send a token of his thanks. Tell him he may send his thank you to the office, and we will see that the correct person receives it. Don't even tell the caller which days or which hours the staff member works. In a world of weirdos everyone is suspect. That could include live-ins, spouses, neighbors, and other family members. Deliver a message about the call to the staff member.

Our rule is absolute: No personal information about any employee may be told by anyone except by that employee.

Patient Problem Number 8:
A patient wants work done and is now "in collections."

The receptionist will refuse credit to this person and refuse service to be rendered until the intended service is prepaid. Chairsides will learn this from the patient care form. Many times reception staff will spot the flagged warning on the care form and inform the patient of our policy.

Burn us once, shame on the patient. Burn us twice, shame on us.

Patient Problem Number 9:
Patient wants his X-rays or copies of his records.

There are laws covering the care and disposition of records and X-rays. Sometimes lay people misunderstand the laws. Our role is to help the patient learn their own rights and know ours.

All original X-rays stay in the office. A copy of a patient ledger may be given to any patient who asks. Simply print the ledger notes only and hand them over. Be sure you give a record only to the patient or to a legal guardian. Patient records may not be sent to a person other than the one named on the record, unless a release of information form is signed by the patient.

If an attorney writes to ask for records, and encloses a patient release, be sure complete records are sent. In this instance, send a copy of the ledger, and copies of clinical notes, tooth and perio charts, the health questionnaire, and all release forms signed by the patient.

Whenever questions about records arise, always make thorough ledger notes that tell who asked for what and why, if you can learn the reason. Patients need not give a reason to obtain their own records, which is another reason to be certain your ledger notations accurately explain treatments and account activity.

According to Iowa law, X-rays are owned by our office, not by a patient. Under no circumstances allow X-rays to leave the office. When a patient asks for his X-rays, tell him that Iowa law requires that we keep the originals. We will be happy to make him a copy and the copying fee is the same as the original cost of the X-ray.

If an attorney asks for a copy of an X-ray and presents a release form, he may have copies at the cost of the original X-ray. If another dentist asks for a patient's X-rays, send copies, not the originals. We do not charge another dentist.

If the State Board of Dental Examiners asks for an X-ray, send copies only, not the originals. In this regard, the Iowa Dental Practice Act states that patient records must be kept for seven years. A record, by legal definition, is a written document. An X-ray, of course, is not a record.

Therefore, X-rays need only be kept through the course of treatment. Prudence dictates, however, that X-rays be kept at least until the expiration of the three-year statute of limitations. There are exceptions, which mandate that we archive X-rays beyond three years.

PATIENT PROBLEM NUMBER 10:
PATIENT (OR A CALLER)
WANTS US TO
DONATE TO A CHARITY
(OR BUY AN ADVERTISING PROGRAM).

Answer to request for donation:

"Office donations are scheduled a year in advance. We will be happy to place your request for donation under consideration for next year."

If the caller persists, he or she may be told that our office conducts two major charities each year, the Doctors With A Heart free dental care and the Senior Citizens Thanksgiving Day Dinner. We ask for no donations to either of these programs, supporting them entirely ourselves. Since they are quite large undertakings there is little left in our gift-giving budget for additional charities.

We do not donate to any telephone solicitation. We donate only to bona fide charities that have submitted documentation of worthiness. Even then, we do not support everyone's pet charity, even those of long-standing patients.

We will donate a handful of toothbrushes to any seemingly legitimate cause—church, school, orphanage, and the like.

Answer to request for advertising dollars: Our ad budgets are set a year in advance. Our advertising committee will be happy to consider your request for next year. Please send us information so we can give it a fair assessment.

If the caller persists by saying he or she wants to personally present the plan, tell the caller personal presentations can only come after the committee has reviewed the program. If the caller chooses not to submit, that is his or her option.

PATIENT PROBLEM NUMBER 11:
A CALLER WISHES TO
SPEAK WITH A DOCTOR,
OR A STAFF MEMBER.

Answer: If the caller wishes to speak with a doctor, ask if it concerns a patient matter so the doctor can review the ledger prior to answering. Obtain an address or a birthdate to be sure you have the correct patient.

If the caller states it is a personal matter, check to see if the doctor is free to visit at that time. If not, inform the caller and ask for a callback number. Place a mailbox notation in the doctor's mailbox, or if the message has a sense of urgency about it, either leave a message on the doctor's desk or inform a chairside so she can pass along the information at an appropriate time.

If the caller wishes to speak with a staff member other than the doctor, take a message and mailbox the recipient, telling the caller that the staff member is occupied but will return the call during a break. Do not forward any but emergency calls into work areas.

Patient Problem Number 12:
Patient says he will pay the balance at the conclusion of his service.

No one except a receptionist can make this determination. This patient may be in bankruptcy, have no job, no money, and have written bad checks before. He may be in collection from several sources. No one except the receptionist who has checked his credit knows these facts.

If she discovers red flags about his creditworthiness, she may raise precautions that allow the office to receive fair pay for fair service. Of course, the usual payments at preparation are enforced. She will check his credit card, run his check through the scanner to determine if there are funds to cover it, or require payment prior to procedure. These efforts are not to thwart the delivery of service, but are designed to assure that payment will be timely.

Patient Problem Number 13:
Patient refuses doctor's examination at hygiene appointment.

This attitude may be acceptable if the patient is being seen on a time span of less than six months. The doctor must approve and it is his decision. Barring his approval, or if the recall is a routine six- or 12-month recall, an exam must be performed.

The patient is to be told, "The standard of care to which this office is held by law requires an examination by a dentist." If the patient refuses, do not reappoint him and tell him nicely that you will miss him.

PATIENT PROBLEM NUMBER 14: FREQUENTLY ASKED QUESTIONS.

Patients ask many questions, because much of what we do contains some mystery. Our goal, of course, is to shed the shroud of mystique that surrounds what we do so our patients can make informed decisions, comfortable with having been told the truth in understandable terms.

There is another reason to answer questions well: The caller may be weighing whether or not to first appoint with us. Easy and nonthreatening answers may inspire that caller to make and keep an appointment with us. The stakes are high. Our jobs demand a new patient flow for this practice to continue our employment.

Some patients may call several times to ask the same question of a different respondent. Our answers must not only be truthful, easy to understand, and address the point, but they must be consistent, as well. Nothing undermines an already apprehensive patient population like an assortment of conflicting answers to the same question.

To obtain consistency in our GD answers to the following patient questions, each staff member is required to commit these answers to memory and to use them each and every time. Just as with patient problems, don't freelance by creating your own answers. These answers work and have been created by the doctors to best represent the GD position on these important matters.

1. Do you allow payments?

Yes, and we accept all major credit cards. Gentle Dental also has an interest-free payment account available for qualified patients. What time of day works best for you?

2. Do you accept dental insurance?

Yes, and we submit insurance for our patients. We accept the insured portion as payment in full. The patient portion is arranged for at each appointment. What time of day works best for you?

3. How much are cleanings?

Cleanings begin at $_____ for children and $_____ for adults. There is a $___ exam fee. What time of day works best for you?

4. How much are fillings?

A simple filling begins at $____. (Use the smallest fee charged.) What time of day works best for you?

5. How much are crowns?

A metal crown begins at $____. What time of day works best for you?

6. How much are dentures?

An economy denture begins at $____. What time of day works best for you?

7. How much are extractions?

A simple extraction begins at $____. What time of day works best for you?

8. How much are root canal fillings?

A single canal can be filled for $____. What time of day works best for you?

9. Do you accept Title XIX patients?

Yes. How soon would you like to be seen?

10. When should children start coming to the dentist?

At age two and a half. By then they have all their primary teeth. What day works best for you?

11. What shall I do to prepare my child to see the dentist?

Nothing. Prepare him no more than when you first took him to the mall. Our staff does an expert job of introducing children to dentistry. Our doctors recommend that new child patients be appointed an hour after breakfast. (Also extremely apprehensive adults!) At that time of day he has had a good night's sleep and his blood sugar is high, all of which help him handle the situation. Which day is most convenient for you?

12. How soon after an extraction can I eat or smoke?

Our doctors advise not eating until the anesthetic wears off and not smoking or drinking colas for 24 hours.

13. Do you put people out for extractions?

No, but we have happy gas available and this makes the experience go far more easily. What time of day is most convenient for you?

14. Do you give second opinions?

Yes, we give free second opinions. What time of day is most convenient for you?

Notice two things about these questions and answers. One, fees are always quoted as the least expensive for that service. Quoting the most expensive crown, denture, or extraction only creates barriers. The patients will be told, in due time, if their needs surpass the simple.

Even quoting a range of fees creates a barrier in the caller's mind. For example, when a patient asks how much a filling is, we could say, "Our fillings range from $50 to $500."

If we said that we would scare the prospective patient away, for he will remember only one thing, $500. We will never see this patient as a patient at Gentle Dental, for we have put the fear of fee in him.

It is not lying or deceptive to quote the beginning fee. But remember, we can never reveal how great we are if callers never make and keep appointments with us. The goal is to make an appointment.

That brings up the second point. You can tell by the question asked if your questioner is sounding you out to determine whether to make an appointment. Make it easy for the caller. Offer to make an appointment. Notice how these questions are phrased.

If you asked, "Do you want to make an appointment?" you have given the caller an easy yes/no answer, and no is always easier to say than yes. A question that requires a yes/no answer is exactly the wrong way to bring people into the office.

Ask instead, "What day works best for you?" Or "What time would fit your schedule best?" These questions presume the caller will make an appointment, and you have made it easier to choose an hour or a day than to say, "No."

NO RX. NO DX.
NO ADVICE GIVEN. NEVER.

There is one further precaution about coping with the unusual. A caller may lead you into diagnosing, prescribing, or giving professional advice. Don't fall into that trap for the consequences could cost you more than your job.

Do not second-guess the doctor by telling the patient what you think the problem might be. Do not prescribe so much as an aspirin, salt water mouthrinse, a toothpick, or a mouthwash. Do not advise the patient to do anything other than come quickly to the office to be seen, or at a minimum, visit with the doctor on the phone. Even saying the problem doesn't seem to require a doctor's attention is diagnosing and could lead to dire problems, for the patient, for the doctor, for the office, and it is guaranteed, for you, too.

When a patient calls post-op, let the doctor handle it. He or she knows what to say. Most any advice you give, except either, "Come right in" or "Doctor will call you," would be wrong. If the doctor has left for the day, someone has the duty 24 hours a day, 365 days a year.

The counsel offered on these pages is offered in the spirit of making the practice of dentistry more fun. That was the goal.

INDEX

R

Recall, 19, 20, 76, 83, 86, 91–93, 96, 97, 100, 103, 136, 140

Receptionist, 11, 12, 14, 59, 86, 95, 112, 113, 119, 129, 180, 183–185,188

Reference check, 31, 172

Referral tracker, 96, 102, 103

Right-brain, 82, 84, 85, 91, 92, 97, 112, 126, 146, 148

S

Safabakhsh, Masih, 114

Scheduler, 92, 93, 95

Schmidt, Catherine, 68, 114
Cathy, 69–75

Screening interview, 25

Seashore, Carl, 58

Signage, 100, 102

Small Claims court, 132

Smart machines, 80, 126

Software, 11, 23, 79, 94, 96, 97, 111, 119, 121

Sooper, 11, 12, 14, 17, 20, 21, 63, 148

Space maintainers, 99, 133

Staff happiness, 17

Staff meetings, 49, 56, 57, 144, 163

Staff rewards, 53, 66

Statement of knowledge, 37, 42, 66

Supplier, 14, 121, 150

Suspension, 62

Systems-driven, 83, 126

T

Tae-Kwon-Do Karate, 13

Team, 5, 7, 10, 12, 16, 17, 19, 21, 22, 24–26, 28, 31, 42, 49, 53, 55–57, 59, 65, 66, 75–77, 98, 110, 149–151, 161, 162, 166

Teamwork, 21, 55, 75, 77, 92

Technicians, 22, 23, 158

Thanksgiving Day dinner, 100

Three-year-olds, 19, 20

Time & Temp, 104

Time & Temperature, 100, 103, 104, 106, 126

Time clock, 24, 121, 126

TMJ, 62

Todd, Kathleen, 73

Toothbrushes, 15, 16, 103, 187

Training manual, 56, 57, 92

Treatment plan, 57, 58, 91, 97, 109, 114, 120, 131, 138, 153, 157, 176

TP, 97, 98, 109, 131

Trial period, 30, 164, 172

Tylenol 3, 60, 62

U

U.S. Department of Commerce, 122, 169

Uncollectible, 132

Unemployment pay, 63, 64

United Way, 16